debut theatre company in association with **Louise Chantal and Paul Deavin**, presents

SNOWBOUND

by **Ciaran McConville**

First performed at Trafalgar Studios, London on 12 March 2008

SNOWBOUND
by **Ciaran McConville**

Cast in order of appearance

Tom	**Sam Hazeldine**
Alex	**Karl Davies**
Mary	**Katherine Manners**
Gerry	**Patrick Brennan**
Janet	**Deborah Thomas**
Clara	**Linda Broughton**
Sally	**Sarah Beck Mather**

Director	**Samantha Potter**
Designer	**Kerry Bradley**
Lighting	**Nick Flintoff**
Sound	**Steve Mayo**
Stage Manager	**Lynsey Fraser**
Assistant Director	**Tim Digby-Bell**
Fight Director	**David Broughton Davies**
Photographer	**Nobby Clark**

Producers	**Louise Chantal**
	Paul Deavin
	Elizabeth Park (for Debut Theatre Company)

Snowbound was given a rehearsed reading at the National Theatre Studio on 14 October 2005.

The play is set between December 1997 and March 2008, in a town on the far edge of the commuter belt in South East England.

The performance lasts approximately one hour and forty-five minutes.

There will be one interval of fifteen minutes.

Debut Theatre Company was founded by Elizabeth Park and Ciaran McConville in 2000 and is based at New Greenham Arts in Newbury, Berkshire. We set out to create exciting ensemble theatre, with a particular focus on new writing and new adaptations.

Snowbound is Debut's eleventh production. Last year we toured Ciaran McConville's one-woman play *These Four Walls* to studio theatres and schools. We have also taken seven productions to the Edinburgh Festival Fringe, several of which transferred to London. Among these were a new adaptation of *Nineteen Eighty Four* (Guardian Critics' Choice), and our new plays: *Immortal, Touched by Fire,* and *The Man Who Dreamed* (Sunday Times Critics' Choice). In 2005 we produced *Christmas Lunch,* a collection of seasonal new writing at the King's Head Theatre in Islington.

In addition to our full productions we hold rehearsed readings and create education packages to accompany many of our productions, and in January this year were awarded charitable status. Our future plans include a tour of *These Four Walls* in 2009.

We hope you enjoy *Snowbound.* If you have any comments, we'd be delighted to hear them!

And if you'd like to stay in touch we'd love you to join our mailing list.
Email us at mailinglist@debut-theatre.org.uk.

'As comical as it is haunting... Debut Theatre Company's production maintains a perfect balance of humour and urgency throughout.'
Time Out

Deborah Thomas

Karl Davies

Katherine Manners and
Sam Hazeldine

CAST

Patrick Brennan

Patrick trained at Central. Theatre includes: for the NT: *The Reporter*, *Light Shining in Buckinghamshire*, *Schism in England*, *Entertaining Strangers*, *Anthony and Cleopatra*, *King Lear*. For the RSC: *Romeo and Juliet*, *Hamlet*, *A Clockwork Orange*. Also: *Guys and Dolls* (Donmar at Piccadilly), *Richard II*, *Edward II*, *Twelfth Night*, *Macbeth*, *Antony and Cleopatra*, *Measure for Measure*, *In Extremis* (Shakespeare's Globe), *Shadow of a Gunman* (Tricycle), *Electricity*, *Macbeth*, *Don Juan* (West Yorkshire Playhouse) *Outside Edge* (New Vic, Staffs) *Tempest* (Derby Playhouse), *Richard III*, *King Lear*, *Taming of the Shrew* (Ludlow Festival), *Fire Raisers*, *Casement* (Riverside Studios), *Glengarry Glen Ross*, *Absurd Person Singular* (Wolsey, Ipswich), *I am Joseph Stalin* (White Bear) *Under Milk Wood* (Bristol Old Vic), *Worlds Apart* (Stratford East), *Twelfth Night* (Liverpool Playhouse), *Merchant of Venice* (Sherman, Cardiff), *Threepenny Opera* (Hi Jinx, Cardiff), *Best Years of Our Lives* (Made in Wales), *Song From a Forgotten City* (UK Tour), *Crimes of the Heart* (Phoenix, Leicester), *Some Kind of Hero*, *Silicon Alley* (Nottingham Playhouse), *Hairy Ape* (Bolton, Octagon). Television includes: *State of Play*, *Casualty*, *Caerdydd*, *Cadfael*, *Wing and a Prayer*, *The Bill*, *Midsomer Murders*, *Nightshift*, *Order out of Chaos*, *In The Company of Strangers*, *Holby City*, *Without Motive*, *Doctors*, *EastEnders*, *Coronation Street*, *The Captain Bligh Conspiracies*, BBC and Globe live broadcasts of *Richard II* and *Measure for Measure*. Plus *The Animated Shakespeare* and *Bible Stories*.
Film: *Franklyn*. Radio: Numerous broadcasts for BBC Radio including *King Lear* live from the Globe for the World Service and most recently *Seven Wonders of the Divided World* for Radio 3.

Linda Broughton

Linda's theatre credits include: Jean in *I like Mine With a Kiss* (Bush); Esther in *The Safari Party* (New Vic Theatre, Stoke); Mrs Sarti in *The Life of Galileo*, Ann Putnam and Sarah Good in *The Crucible*, Heather in *Racing Demon*, Gwenda in *Absence of War* and *Murmuring Judges* (all at Birmingham Rep); Sylvia in *Ballroom* for De Le Warr Pavillion (Tour); Pam in *Hoxton Story* (the Red Room); Miss Prism in *The Importance of Being Earnest* (Royal Theatre, Northampton); *When the Wind Blows* (Southwark Playhouse); *Northanger Abbey* and *Forty Years On* (Northcott, Exeter); *Sugar Dollies* (The Gate); *My Mother Said I Never Should* (Royal Theatre, Northampton); *Rookery Nook* (Greenwich Theatre); *Small Poppies* (Young Vic); *Macbeth* (Crucible, Sheffield); *Caucasian Chalk Circle* (Birmingham Rep). In the seventies, Linda was a founder member of Monstrous Regiments and toured with them in *Scum* and *Vinegar Tom*. Currently she is a member of The Factory and a regular in their ongoing performances of *Hamlet*.
Television includes: *Waking The Dead*, *Casualty*, *Paul Merton: Does China Exist?*, *Hetty Wainthropp Investigates*, *Fist of Fun*, *Chandler and Co.*, *Roughnecks*, *Doctors*, *Knowing Me Knowing You* and *A Dark Adapted Eye* (all for the BBC); *Carrie and Barry* and *Men Behaving Badly* (Hartswood Films); *Wycliffe* (HTV); *Expert Witness* (LWT); *The Bill* (Thames); *Firm Friends* (Zenith); *How We Used to Live* (Yorkshire Television).
Film includes: *Babel* (GMH Films Ltd); *Bridget Jones's Diary* (Working Title); *Sliding Doors* (Sliding Doors Productions); *Watch That Man* (Luna Pictures). Recent radio includes: *Untitled Love* (BBC World Service), *The Two Pipe Problem* and *The Card* (Catherine Bailey productions).

Karl Davies

Karl started acting with a local theatre group in Stockport at the age of seven. His first first professional role, a part in *Peak Practice*, came at the age of sixteen, whilst he was doing his A-levels. Karl then went on to appear in *Fat Friends* (ITV), *The Bill* (ITV), a US drama called *The Hidden City*, *Emmerdale* (ITV), *Dead Clever* (ITV), *A Very British Sex Scandal* (Channel 4) and *Kingdom* (ITV). His first film role was in a short called *Me And Her*, which was followed by an appearance in the feature *Dolphins*, which is yet to be completed. Karl's first stage role was last year, in Tim Firth's *Flint Street Nativity*, at the Liverpool Playhouse.

Sam Hazeldine

Sam trained at RADA. Theatre includes: *Othello*, (Salisbury Theatre), *Hamlet* (English Touring Theatre), *Blues for Mister Charlie* (Tricycle Theatre). TV includes: *The Bill* (ITV), *Persuasion* (ITV), *Midsomer Murders* (ITV), *Life on Mars* (BBC), *Foyle's War* (ITV), *Shameless* (Channel Four). Film includes: *Chromophobia* (Martha Fiennes), *Bridget Jones: The Edge of Reason* (Working Title).

Katherine Manners

Theatre includes: *Coram Boy* (both seasons), *The House of Bernarda Alba*, *Cyrano de Bergerac*, *The Prime of Miss Jean Brodie* (all National Theatre); *King Lear* (RSC Academy); *The Master Builder* (West End); *Amadeus*, *Dracula* (both Derby Playhouse); *War* (Strindberg's Intima Theater, Stockholm), *I am a Superhero* (Old Vic/503 New Voices award). Television includes: *Doctors*, *Casualty*.

Sarah Beck Mather

Sarah trained at the Central School of Speech and Drama. Credits whilst at Drama School include *As You Like It*, *Richard II*, *Children of the Sun*, *Barbarians*, *Orpheus Descending*, *The Man of Mode*, *The Libertine* and *The Rimers of Eldritch*. Television includes *The Bill* and *The Royal*.

Deborah Thomas

Deborah trained at Arts Ed. Theatre includes: *A Midsummer Night's Dream*, (tour of India); *The Settling Dust* (Union Theatre); *How Many Ducks In Stacey* (Union Theatre); *Eclipsed* (Tabard Theatre); *The Dutch Courtesan* (Tabard Theatre); *Pack Of Lies* (Malvern).

CREATIVE TEAM

Kerry Bradley Designer

Kerry trained at the University of Warwick, Bristol Old Vic Theatre School and the National Film and Television School. She progressed from Design and Wardrobe assistant to Resident Designer at the Swan Theatre, Worcester and Palace Theatre, Westcliff. She became freelance on moving to London 13 years ago. She is currently Associate Lecturer at Wimbledon School of Art and works mostly as a Theatre designer and Buyer in Television and Film.

This is Kerry's first design for Debut Theatre Company. She also designed *Heroes* for Samantha Potter last year (National Theatre). She has designed many new (and old) plays throughout London and on tour. Recent designs include *Growing Up an Alien* (Apples & Snakes) and *Romeo and Juliet* (The Lord Chamberlain's Men). She has also worked for RADA, Leicester Haymarket, Pop-Up Theatre, Snap Theatre, Polka Theatre (Wimbledon) and London Bubble. Recent work as a Production Buyer and Set Dresser: *Jim, Jam & Sunny* (Wish Films), *Dolphins* (Carnaby Films), *Footballers' Wives' TV* (Shed TV).

David Broughton Davies
Fight Director

David trained at the Royal Welsh College of Music and Drama. He became an Associate Member of the Society of British Fight Directors whilst teaching stage combat at Cygnet Drama Training, Exeter and the Aarhus Theatr Akedemi, Denmark.

David has choreographed, performed and fight captained staged combat, armed and unarmed, as far afield as Stockholm, Chicago and Southwark. He has performed with companies such as the RSC, ESC, Royal Theatre Northampton, Theatr Clwyd, Sherman Theatre Cardiff, Vienna's English speaking theatre, Ludlow festival, Steppenwolf Chicago and the National Theatre's Education Department.

David has just completed work on the latest Jacqueline Wilson adaptation of *Secrets*, which recently opened at the Polka Theatre in Wimbledon. He is pleased to be working with Samantha Potter again after *Sparkleshark* and *Arden at Faversham*.

Louise Chantal Producer

Louise Chantal produces new and international theatre in the UK and abroad and until recently was the theatre producer at Assembly Theatres and the Riverside Studios in London. Louise was previously awarded two prestigious New Producer Bursaries from Stage One and the Society of London Theatres (2004/5). Recent theatre productions include *Forgotten Voices* (with Matthew Kelly and Belinda Lang); *Midnight Cowboy* (world premiere); *The Exonerated* at the Riverside Studios, Edinburgh Festival and Dublin International Theatre Festival (cast members included Aidan Quinn, Stockard Channing, Danny Glover, Kristin Davis, Mackenzie Crook, Alanis Morrissette and Catherine Tate); *The Odd Couple* with Bill Bailey and Alan Davies (Edinburgh 2005); *Thom Pain (based on nothing)* at Edinburgh, London and New York (Pulitzer Prize finalist 2005); and work with the multi-award winning American company The Riot Group worldwide. www.chantalarts.co.uk

Tim Digby-Bell Assistant Director

Tim graduated from Edinburgh University in 2005. He completed a year's internship with Nica Burns at Nimax Theatres in the West End before working as Assistant Director on their UK Tour of *One Flew over the Cuckoo's Nest*. He formed Talac Theatre in early 2007 and wrote and directed their first piece, *Short Stories*, at the Hen and Chickens in Islington. Their second, *Tell*, which he wrote and directed, premiered at the Underbelly at the Edinburgh Festival before transferring to the New End Theatre in Hampstead to critical acclaim. While in Edinburgh he also worked for the If Comedy awards, scouting comedy shows. He is currently writing the next play for Talac Theatre which he will direct later on this year. He is also one half of the electronic-rock band *Duologue*.

Nick Flintoff *Lighting Designer*

Nick trained at RADA before running the technical department at the Gantry in Southampton. From there, he began working for Imagination Ltd as a full time Production Manager and then he joined their Lighting Design team working on various large scale projects. Leaving the Corporate World, Nick returned to theatre, where he now works at the Corn Exchange in Newbury. He has recently lit tours for such names as David Benson, Barb Jingr, Richard Thomson's Rebus MacTaggart, Plested & Brown, Piggynero and not to forget the local pantomime. Nick is also writing a six part fantasy children's television series which is currently in development. After lighting Debut's tour of *These Four Walls*, Nick is delighted to be asked back a second time, to work on this production of *Snowbound*.

Lynsey Fraser *Stage Manager*

Lynsey studied Stage Management at the Central School of Speech and Drama, and graduated with BA (Hons) in Theatre Practice. Her most recent work includes *Sleeping Beauty* for UK Productions, *The Ugly One* at The Royal Court and *Monster* and *Things of Dry Hours* at The Royal Exchange Manchester. She has worked for theatre companies such as RASA, Rifco Arts, Peckham Arts and The Gate, including productions at the New Players Theatre and the Ovalhouse. Theatre credits for Debut Theatre Company include *Nineteen Eighty Four*, *Shostakovich* and *These Four Walls*.

Ciaran McConville *Writer*

Ciaran trained as an actor at Arts Ed. Writing for the stage includes: *The Settling Dust*, *These Four Walls*, *Shostakovich*, *Touched by Fire*, *Immortal* and *The Man Who Dreamed*. Adaptations include *Nineteen Eighty Four*, *The Gift of the Magi* and, for children, *Oliver Twist* and *Frankenstein*. Other children's plays include *Pip's War*.

As an actor, theatre includes *Horrible Histories* (Birmingham Stage Company), *Pride & Prejudice* (Illyria), *You Never Can Tell* (Peter Hall Company) and *The Things Good Men Do* (Lyric Hammersmith). Radio includes *Left* for BBC Radio 4.

Ciaran is a founding director of Debut Theatre Company. He is appearing in *Sound Dust* at Theatre 503 from 18 to 22 March 2008.

Samantha Potter *Director*

Samantha trained at Dartington College of Arts and the National Theatre Studio. Directing credits include: *In Spitting Distance* (NT Platform), *S**t-Mix* (NT Studio), *Peapickers* (Eastern Angles Regional Tour), *Heroes* (National Theatre Education Tour), *Cosi Fan Tutte* (Glyndebourne on Tour- Revival Director), *Arden of Faversham* (White Bear Theatre), *Cose Fan Tutte* (BBC Proms at the Royal Albert Hall), *Liquid* (Tristan Bates Theatre), *The Head of Red O'Brien* (Oran Mor, Glasgow), *A Sexual Congress* (NT Platform) and *Don Juan Comes Back from the War* (Courtyard Theatre). Samantha's work at the National Theatre includes Associate Director on *Paul* (dir. Howard Davies), and Staff Director on *Henry IV: Parts 1 and 2* (dir. Nicholas Hytner), *Buried Child* (dir. Matthew Warchus), *Cyrano de Bergerac* (dir. Howard Davies), *Tales from the Vienna Woods* (dir. Richard Jones). Her work for the RSC includes Assistant Director on *Coriolanus*, *The Merry Wives of Windsor* and *The Prisoner's Dilemma*.

Samantha teaches at LAMDA, Mountview and E15 drama schools and reads scripts for the Soho Theatre and the NT.

This production of *Snowbound* has been made possible by the generous support of the following organisations:

*Life*SEARCH

ACKNOWLEDGEMENTS

Supporters

Babs & Peter Thomas
Sylvia Argyle, Jessica Boyd, Alex Boyd-Williams, James Daley, Kieren Daley, Caroline Dow, Neal Foster, Nathan Francis, Sam Fraser, Penny Griffin, Jamie Harper, Olga Harper, Melanie Hill, Shirley Hill, Sally Hunter, Tim Hyam, Chris Jackson, Keith & Linda James, Andre Mansi, Sarah Marsden, Chris Moss, Simon Nock, Mark & Judi Nurcombe, Ayo Oyebade, Nick & Jane Park, Chris Prickett, Wilf & Anne Sutton, Andy Thomas, Stan Thomas, Jen York

Actors who assisted in development

Kate Best, Isla Blair, Trevor Cooper, Chris Courtenay, Olivia Darnley, Morgan Dear, Lorna Doyle, Olivia Hallinan, Richard Heap, Ellie Howell, Sally Hunter, Tom Jude, Marianna Maniatakis, Anna Maxwell-Martin, Pamela Merrick, Ingrid Oliver, Luanna Priestman, Nick Sidi, Emma Stansfield, Darren Tighe, Lucy Tregear, Rob Wynne.

Thanks to

Jack Bradley, Miriam Buether, Lucy Davies, Katy Griffiths, Giles Harrison, Hywel John, Brigid Larmour, Clare Lawrence, Nicky Lund, Kate McGregor, Michael Mears, Katie Mitchell, Dan Muirden, Hamish Pirie, Matthew Poxon, Gavin Ricketts, Matthew Scott, Sandra and John White, Ambassador Theatre Group, Birmingham Stage Company, Freecycle, Jez at Gerriets, Dee at A.S.Homecare, National Theatre, NT Studio, Newbury Corn Exchange and New Greenham Arts, the staff and students of Alleyn's School and Rosendale Primary School, Richard and Wes at De Novo Events, Hampshire, Rylaux Carpets (www.ryalux.com), Lizzie Bardell, Oliver Gray, Andrew Visnevski, James Seabright and Kat Portman at Seabright Productions, Sean Hinds.

Special thanks to

John Cannon, James Daley, Sarah Marsden, Luanna Priestman, Will Rycroft

Finally, thanks to the many people who will have helped after this goes to print.

 The carpet featured in the play was kindly donated by Pownall Carpets. www.pownallcarpets.com

The crockery and glasses in the play were kindly supplied by The Denby Pottery Co. Ltd.

Alleyn's School
Drama Department

Trafalgar Studios

'A revolution for the West End'

Trafalgar Studios is one of London's most exciting theatre venues, renowned for its innovative and cutting edge productions. Since this unique venue opened in 2003, audiences have had the chance to see exceptional theatre that doesn't take place anywhere else in the West End.

Trafalgar Studios consists of two dynamic perform-ance spaces. The larger space, Studio 1, was launched in 2003 and created from the original art deco auditorium of the Whitehall Theatre, ▶ and the intimate 100 seat Studio 2 opened in 2005 and is the first of its kind in the West End. ▼

Photography by JR

The award winning work presented at Trafalgar Studios receives both national and inter-national acclaim, and offers audiences theatre that is fresh, stimulating and challenging.

In addition to its varied production seasons, Trafalgar Studios presents a diverse and eclectic programme of play-readings, late night events, exclusive gigs, stand up comedy, film screenings, theatre tours and educational workshops.

Book online and find out more at
www.theambassadors.com/trafalgarstudios

SNOWBOUND

First published in 2008 by Oberon Books Ltd
521 Caledonian Road, London N7 9RH
Tel: 020 7607 3637 / Fax: 020 7607 3629
e-mail: info@oberonbooks.com
www.oberonbooks.com

A catalogue record for this book is available from the British
Library.

ISBN: 978-1-84002-847-8

Cover photograph by Nobby Clark

Printed in Great Britain by Antony Rowe Ltd, Chippenham.

Characters

TOM   *born 1972*

ALEX   *born 1974*

SALLY   *born 1975*

MARY   *born 1975*

CLARA   *born 1947*

GERRY   *born 1956*

JANET   *born 1967*

The play is set in a town on the far edge of the commuter belt in South East England, between December 1997 and March 2008.

A forward slash (/) in the dialogue denotes a point of interruption.

This text went to press before the end of rehearsals and so may differ slightly from the play as performed.

For Sam Potter

ACT ONE
DIFFICULT QUESTIONS

Two brothers meet in an embrace.

In the distance a train screams through the night.

TOM: Alright, Alex. Alright. Come on. Deep breaths. What do we say?

ALEX: One –

TOM: Keep breathing. Keep breathing, Alex.

ALEX: One, two –

TOM: That's it. Slowly.

ALEX: One, two, three, four, five, / six, seven, eight, nine, ten.

TOM: Six, seven, eight, nine, ten. All done.

ALEX: No. (*Panicking again.*) Got to –

TOM: Alright.

ALEX: Got to to to –

TOM: Got to listen.

ALEX: Listen.

TOM: Got to focus.

ALEX: Focus.

TOM: What can you hear?

ALEX: Too much.

TOM: No, one thing.

ALEX: Hear the train.

TOM: That's right. The train.

ALEX: Out there. In the dark.

TOM: The train, heading out of town. Same time, every night.

ALEX: It's late tonight.

TOM: Can you imagine it, picture it?

ALEX: Yes.

TOM: Tell me about the train, Alex.

ALEX: See the lights.

TOM: What do they look like, the lights?

ALEX: Yellow. Blazing past trees. Streak of light.

TOM: Is that what it is?

ALEX: Streak of light in the dark. (*Panic rising.*) Howling.

TOM: One thing. Listen.

ALEX: People on the train.

TOM: You can hear the people on the train?

ALEX: I can see them. Too many.

TOM: One person. Someone different from last time.

ALEX: A girl.

TOM: Tell me about the girl.

ALEX: Smiling.

TOM: She's thinking about someone.

ALEX: Someone she loves.

TOM: A man?

ALEX: Must be.

TOM: Maybe she's thinking about me.

ALEX: On her way to see him. Loves him.

TOM: That's something to smile about.

The sound of the train disappears. There's a silence.

ALEX: It's gone.

TOM: The train?

ALEX: Dark now.

TOM: Life goes on.

ALEX: In darkness?

TOM: Yes. All done. Just you and me.

ALEX: That's what it always is.

TOM: That's what matters.

ALEX: Don't let go.

TOM: Bad dream?

ALEX: Yes.

TOM: Want to talk about it?

ALEX: Dreamt about Mum.

TOM: Is that what it was?

ALEX: Dreamt she was here.

TOM: She's not here, Alex.

ALEX: Do you dream about her?

TOM: It's different for me.

ALEX: Will it ever stop?

TOM: I hope so. Some day.

ALEX: When I'm awake, you know, she's happy. There's a warmth. But when I'm asleep it's like I open my eyes and she's just there. Angry.

TOM: What would she have to be angry about?

ALEX: Me. Angry with me.

TOM: That's your imagination.

ALEX: She loved you.

TOM: She loved us all.

ALEX: Why wasn't she happy, then?

TOM: I don't know the answer to that.

ALEX: Doesn't love make you happy?

TOM: Like your girl on the train?

17

ALEX: Don't know, made her up.

TOM: Mum used to say, 'We're made strong by the people we love.'

ALEX: Made strong?

TOM: Like you can withstand anything.

ALEX: Like iron?

TOM: We're forged, like iron.

ALEX: Like rock?

TOM: We're hewn, like rock.

ALEX: Hewn…

TOM: Pretty good, huh?

ALEX: We're not rocks.

TOM: Alex, it's a figure of speech. You know that, you joker.

ALEX: Strong is different from happy. So why wasn't Mum strong?

TOM: It's late now.

ALEX: One question.

TOM: It's never one question.

ALEX: One question, then bed.

TOM: There isn't a simple answer.

ALEX: But there is an answer?

TOM: To what?

ALEX: To what love makes you feel. To what it makes you do.

TOM: I don't know. I don't know if there's an answer to that.

ALEX: I love you.

TOM: And I love you.

ALEX: And we're happy.

TOM: We do alright, bro. You know what time it is? It's the middle of the night.

ALEX: Never talk about…things. Not really. Sleep in your bed?

TOM: Not tonight.

ALEX: It's dark outside.

TOM: You're snug as a bug.

ALEX: Life goes on in darkness.

TOM: One for the book. Get some sleep, hey? We're seeing the specialist in the morning.

ALEX: Our burden. Not yours. Could share it.

TOM: Where do you get off talking about burdens?

ALEX: Don't want to be your burden.

TOM: Alex, you're my kid brother.

ALEX: Love shouldn't be a burden.

TOM: You're not – Christ, you're not – don't ever say that, okay? I will always – look at me – I will always be around. Okay?

ALEX: I know.

TOM: That beautiful brain of yours. I don't know where you get these ideas.

ALEX: Think too much.

TOM: Yes, you do.

ALEX: Just want to understand things.

TOM: Come here, you soft sod.

ALEX: I think I can go to sleep now.

TOM: It's going to be alright. I can tell.

TOM kisses him on the forehead.

SCENE 2: TOWN IN THE HOME COUNTIES, DECEMBER, 1997

ALEX stands with his arms outstretched, eyes closed and head turned up to the sky.

MARY looks at ALEX, looks up at the sky, and looks at ALEX again.

ALEX: (*To himself.*) Electric.

MARY: Are you expecting someone?

ALEX: Waiting for it to snow.

MARY: It's going to snow? Now?

ALEX: In a few minutes.

MARY: How do you know?

ALEX: Sometimes I can tell when the snow's going to touch my face.

MARY: Can I try?

ALEX: You have to concentrate. Like this. Concentrate.

They concentrate, eyes closed, heads turned up to the sky. Enter TOM, unseen.

Can you feel it?

MARY: I think I can. It's like when you close your eyes and wait to be kissed.

ALEX: Like the air's been sharpened to a point.

MARY: That's quite a talent.

ALEX: My mum used to say that snowflakes were angels. Look at them too closely, they melt away.

TOM: It's not going to snow, Alex.

ALEX: How do you know?

TOM: Michael Fish said so.

ALEX: He's wrong.

TOM: Alex, the man's been wrong once in thirty years. He's the weatherman.

MARY: I'm with Alex.

TOM: Come on, or we'll be late.

ALEX: Nice to meet you.

MARY: And you. I'm going to stay here and wait for the angels.

TOM: (*To ALEX.*) Go sit in the car. I'll catch you up.

ALEX leaves, with the car keys.

MARY: I'm sorry.

TOM: He gets confused.

MARY: I wasn't teasing him. Genuinely.

TOM: There's nothing wrong with him.

MARY: I know.

TOM: But he is a bit mental. Human contact can be, I don't know, overwhelming.

MARY: I agree with him.

TOM: He likes nature. Likes the weather, because it's safe. He can let the weather overwhelm him. People need to be taken on his terms. Or he goes mental.

MARY: What are his terms?

TOM: He can't connect. Too sensitive.

MARY: Like a baby bat.

TOM: Yeah. What?

MARY: Sensitivity is a very unusual quality in a man.

TOM: Actually, he's incredibly articulate.

MARY: Two unusual qualities in a man.

TOM: He'd be the first person to spot if you were pulling his leg.

MARY: I didn't touch him. He was waiting for it to snow. I get that. You don't remember me, do you?

TOM: Mary Martins. You were in my sister's year.

MARY: You do!

TOM: Used to dance in the hall on Tuesday evenings.

MARY: Yes!

TOM: Like an elephant.

MARY: Thank you!

TOM: I could hear you from the other side of the school.

MARY: Course you could.

TOM: You've blossomed. Well, I should go.

MARY: Dance with me.

She begins to dance as if she were at a party and had finished her fourth drink.

TOM: I'm sorry?

MARY: Dance with me.

TOM: Now?

MARY: Why not?

TOM: We need music.

MARY: We don't need music.

TOM: Alright.

He dances as if at a party and tee total.

I haven't noticed you around.

MARY: I haven't been here.

TOM: Where've you been?

MARY: University.

TOM: Since you were fourteen?

MARY: Since I was worth noticing.

TOM: Been back long?

MARY: Arrived last night, my very good man.

TOM: What brought you back?

MARY: Curious to see the old place. Offer some hope. Heal the afflicted. Also, I have nowhere to live. I am currently without abode.

TOM: I've just started college. A little late.

MARY: Never too late. What are you studying?

TOM: Media, whatever that means. Part-time course in London. But things here – well, we'll see. My sister's the brains. You remember Sally?

MARY: I used to copy her homework.

TOM: She's at Oxford. Someone had to stay here, hold the fort.

MARY: And is the fort holding?

TOM: Just about. She's back for Christmas in a few weeks.

MARY: Say hi from me.

TOM: So, what are you going to do?

MARY: You mean when I grow up?

TOM: If and when.

MARY: No idea.

TOM: No idea?

TOM stops dancing.

MARY: Wait for it to snow.

TOM: And when it starts snowing?

MARY: Wait for it to stop.

MARY stops dancing.

TOM: I have to go.

MARY: Did I say something?

TOM: Alex – you know. Don't you ever get sick of this town?

MARY: I just got here.

TOM: I can't stand it.

MARY: It's nice.

TOM: Nice? Nothing happens. I want to see the world. I want to live in Paris and learn French and teach. And then maybe New York. Watch the Yankees. Write a novel. Walk the Appalachians. There's a giant hole in the earth in

Mexico and you just lean over the edge with a parachute and drop down into it. I want to see the Great Barrier Reef. I want to explore Mumbai on foot. I want to unlock secrets.

MARY: So go.

TOM: I can't.

MARY: Why?

TOM: Something always happens.

MARY: Alex?

TOM: When my sister gets back, well I can pick up then.

MARY: I've travelled.

TOM: Yeah?

MARY: Of course. I saw the Lost World of Appapundo. I hiked the mountains of Grepungi. I once shot a Wrinkled Babaquot from four hundred yards. Among certain tribes, I am venerated as a Shaman. I don't remember ever unlocking any secrets that I couldn't unlock here.

TOM: You're laughing at me.

MARY: Only on the inside.

TOM: I'm allowed to dream, aren't I, without your elephant-stamping?

MARY: You've got a runaway eyelash.

TOM: What?

MARY: Sorry. An eyelash. Just here. Do you mind?

TOM: Depends what you're going to do.

MARY: Sorry. I have this thing.

She picks the eyelash from his cheek and holds it on the tip of her finger.

Make a wish.

He does so, and blows the eyelash off her finger.

What did you wish for? What's funny?

TOM: Nothing.

MARY: So, what was it?

TOM: I wished for a white Christmas.

MARY: It won't come true now you've told me.

TOM: Well then why did you ask me?

MARY: I was curious.

TOM: What do you wish for?

MARY: Peace on earth and goodwill toward men.

TOM: What do you really wish for?

MARY: I can't tell you.

TOM: Why not?

MARY: I'd have to kill you.

A car alarm goes off.

TOM: I've got to go.

MARY: Is he okay, do you think?

TOM: It's cold. Can I give you a lift?

MARY: You can call me.

TOM: I haven't got your number.

MARY: You wanted to unlock secrets. Start there.

SCENE 3: GERRY'S HOUSE, DECEMBER, 1997

GERRY, JANET, TOM and ALEX sit around a table. ALEX inspects a new video camera he has just taken out of its box.

GERRY: I hope it's going to help, Alex.

TOM: It's incredibly generous.

ALEX: Thank you, Gerry and Janet.

JANET: Tiny, isn't it? So you can carry it around.

TOM: Every man needs gadgets.

JANET: Why are you so happy?

TOM: Just the Christmas spirit.

GERRY: When something gets too difficult to take in, press record and then play back exactly what it was on the big screen. See it for what it really was. It's going to help, Alex. Help you frame things.

ALEX: Like a picture.

GERRY: Like a manageable picture.

TOM: Worth a try, isn't it? Always take the doctor's advice, right, Gerry?

GERRY: No sign of the fits coming back?

TOM: No. No more grand mal, right?

ALEX: Just panic, occasionally.

JANET: We all panic occasionally.

GERRY: No more grand mal? That's terrific.

TOM: And the new specialist has made some suggestions, hasn't she, bro?

ALEX: Permanent care and a change of medication.

TOM: That's, no, that's not what she suggested, exactly.

GERRY: Permanent care?

TOM: She thought there might be some financial help –

GERRY: And send him to a home?

ALEX: Don't want to move.

TOM: How's Sarah, Janet?

JANET: Fine, thank you. She's full-time at nursery now, and loving it.

GERRY: More drugs? I don't understand – when are they actually going to suggest something –

ALEX: Don't want to move to London.

GERRY: London? Who said London?

TOM: I suggested it. (*To ALEX.*) You're taking things too literally.

GERRY: Tom, leave here?

TOM: It's not good for us here; the town, the house, especially the house.

ALEX: Make Mum angry if we moved.

TOM: For Christ's sake!

JANET: Tom, Sarah's asleep.

TOM: I'm sorry, but this is driving me nuts.

GERRY: Why do you think it would make her angry?

ALEX: Can feel her in the house.

TOM: Alex, it's your imagination. You understand? You've got to learn to, to – oh, Christ, why do I bother?

JANET: Why don't you head off, honey?

TOM: And now the sulk. Look at him. (*To ALEX.*) Look at you!

GERRY: Tom, you head out. You've got your course.

TOM: Yeah, my course. Nice idea. Have I ever finished anything? Have I ever been allowed to finish, achieve, do, do… I'm sorry. I'm sorry.

JANET: It's okay.

TOM: Look after that camera, hey, bro? (*To GERRY and JANET.*) Nine o'clock, then?

GERRY: Why don't you stay the night, Alex?

JANET: Gerry, I don't know –

GERRY: Give Tom a chance to let his hair down.

ALEX: Sleep in my room. My bed.

GERRY: We could make you up a bed.

JANET: Gerry.

TOM: Don't worry about it. I'll see you at nine. Thank you, thank you.

Exit TOM.

GERRY: We like having you here, Alex. It wouldn't be a chore for us. We could have him here the odd night, couldn't we sweetheart?

JANET: Can we talk about that? Let me check on Sarah and you boys can play with your toys.

Exit JANET.

ALEX: Tom doesn't believe me. About Mum.

GERRY: Tom can't see the things you can see. Nor can I.

ALEX: Holding him back.

GERRY: You're not. We've just got to find a way to let Tom do things separately.

ALEX: Camera's a really good present.

GERRY: You can be as creative as you like. The drawings you've exhibited, I think they're fantastic, Alex.

ALEX: I know, in the end, I know I have to let him go.

GERRY: I'm sorry?

ALEX: Let him go. Because that's love, isn't it? Tear myself out of him like ivy, let him breathe, let him live. Not sacrifice.

GERRY: He's not – what sacrifice?

ALEX: Do you help Tom because Mum died?

GERRY: I help because I can.

ALEX: Mum climbed up you like ivy, didn't she?

GERRY: Let's look at this camera. I'm a big believer in reading the manual.

ALEX: Need to understand, if I'm ever going to help, to use, this, my mind, if I am ever going to let Tom go. In my home – what I see, feel, don't understand, Tom won't answer, won't tell me. The decisions we make, are they always because of love?

GERRY: Not always. I eat because I need to survive. I work because I need to make a living.

ALEX: You're a doctor. Your work is love.

GERRY: It's different.

ALEX: Not for me.

GERRY: Well, my brain is able to select, to channel. That's why this camera –

ALEX: How can it be good not to ask questions?

GERRY: Is this about your mum? Alex, the right thing to do is to move on.

ALEX: In my home – please, listen to me – you just have to close your eyes, run your cheek along the wall, she reaches back; she's in the house. But you have to close your eyes. You have to listen, closer. Much closer. All the pain, it's love. Isn't it?

GERRY: Alex –

ALEX: Isn't it?!

GERRY: Alex, you're working yourself into a state. Look at me.

Enter JANET.

JANET: Fast asleep, thank God.

ALEX: Don't want to go to a home.

GERRY: No one's going to –

ALEX: Want my brother. Don't want to, to –

GERRY: Alright, Alex.

ALEX: Can't focus! Too much!

GERRY: Look at me!

ALEX: I don't want to go to a home. I DON'T WANT TO GO TO A HOME I DON'T WANT –

GERRY: Call Tom. Quickly, call Tom!

SCENE 4: MARY AND CLARA'S HOUSE, DECEMBER, 1997

TOM and MARY enter dressed up from a date.

TOM: So this is your place?

MARY: It actually belongs to the Great Sultan. I'm just one of the harem girls. It's a tough life. I spend my afternoons lazing on the chaise-longue, sucking grapes and humming sweet melodies.

TOM: What?

MARY: It's my mum's place, yeah.

TOM: She live here?

MARY: Yes.

TOM: In the walls, or can you actually see her?

MARY: You can actually see her.

TOM: Mind if I use your loo?

MARY: First on the left.

TOM: Don't go away.

> *TOM exits. MARY drapes herself on the sofa and hums a sweet melody. CLARA enters carrying sheet music.*

MARY: Mum!

CLARA: Scared him off, dear?

MARY: He's just – I thought you were going out.

CLARA: I am.

MARY: I mean, I thought you would be gone.

CLARA: How was dinner?

MARY: Alright.

CLARA: Oh dear.

MARY: I don't know how keen he is.

CLARA: Well, you brought him back.

MARY: He walked me home.

CLARA: In my day that meant a damn good –

MARY: When is your lesson?

CLARA: I'm going. (*Getting ready to go out.*) So, what does he do?

MARY: He looks after his brother.

CLARA: Oh, a carer?

MARY: Don't do that, Mum.

CLARA: What? It's good that he's a carer.

MARY: You were insinuating free minibuses and special needs classes at the local library, and spoon-feeding mashed up bananas to his brother.

CLARA: What about all those nice, bright boys at university?

MARY: Morons all.

CLARA: And when he's not mashing bananas, what does he do?

MARY: He's passionate. He just needs a break.

CLARA: He's drifting? Well, that's something you've got in common.

MARY: I'm not drifting, I'm basking in the sunshine of an unwritten future.

CLARA: Well paid, is it?

MARY: They're artists.

CLARA: Who?

MARY: Tom and Alex. You know the exhibition at the library, the drawings?

CLARA: The special needs drawings?

MARY: If you're going to embarrass me –

CLARA: No, I'm glad. I was worried you were a lesbian.

MARY: Be gone!

CLARA: Anyone less than perfect doesn't deserve you.

TOM enters, drying his hands on his jeans.

MARY: Tom, this is Mum.

CLARA: Clara.

TOM: Nice to meet you.

MARY: Right, well you should –

CLARA: Mary tells me you're an artist.

MARY: Alex's exhibition.

TOM: My brother. He's very talented. Incredible detail. Landscapes, on the whole. Portraits are a bit stressful.

CLARA: I must go along and have a look.

MARY: Tell Mum about the filming.

TOM: Oh, Alex was given a camcorder and he's obsessed with it. I'm helping him put together a film.

CLARA: A film?

TOM: Bits and pieces. It sounds absurd to talk about it. But if it works out well, we'll buy some equipment and make another one. Since I've had to give up my course, it's given us something to do.

CLARA: I wish Mary would find something to do.

MARY: Mum thinks I should move out.

TOM: Out of this town, I agree.

CLARA: And where would that leave you?

TOM: Bereft.

MARY: It's settled. I'm staying.

CLARA: I like having her here, really. I don't know what I'd do if she buggered off.

TOM: So, you're a musician?

CLARA: I teach. Mary's father and I were both pianists.

TOM: I didn't know that.

CLARA: We started off playing a duet and ended up on entirely different pieces. It's been lovely to meet you, Tom. Take care of my little girl.

MARY: It's just a date.

CLARA: (*To TOM.*) Are you staying the night?

MARY: Oh, my God!

TOM: I was just, um…

CLARA: I might see you later. Have fun.

TOM: Bye.

CLARA leaves.

MARY: I am really sorry.

TOM: She's great!

MARY: So embarrassing. Parents, huh? Oh, God, I'm sorry -I'm sorry, Tom.

TOM: Don't be daft.

MARY: Drink?

TOM: What you got?

MARY: Scotch?

TOM: Twenty-two going on fifty, huh?

MARY: It's Mum's.

TOM: Lovely, if that's okay…

MARY prepares a couple of whiskies.

MARY: She likes having me here. I think she's been lonely.

TOM: So, your dad –

MARY: Left. When I was tiny. I see him. Cheers.

TOM: Cheers. I think you're mad to stay here. You're smart, you're beautiful – the world is your oyster.

MARY: I hate oysters.

TOM: Why did you come out with me?

MARY: I had a crush on you at school.

TOM: That's it?

MARY: More than a crush.

TOM: We barely knew each other.

MARY: Well, I'm a bit dotty.

TOM: You could have anyone.

MARY: I don't want anyone.

TOM: Mary, if you and I – my brother comes attached, you know? Doesn't that freak you out?

MARY: You probably don't remember, but I came to your mum's funeral.

TOM: I do remember.

MARY: You were hard as a statue. That ferocious look in your eyes. One arm round Sally, the other holding Alex's hand.

TOM: I've never told him. About Mum. The actual… What could I say?

MARY: I know you've had to make decisions, Tom. And I know what you've sacrificed. Like travelling, and college.

TOM: Yeah.

MARY: What about Open University?

TOM: No, I want to get out of here and meet people who don't thrash their arms around if someone gives them the time of day.

MARY: There's me.

TOM: Sally graduates in the summer. I can finally go and spend some time in the land of the living.

MARY: Is that the deal?

TOM: She's a good kid.

MARY: You tell me I should see the world, why don't you want the same for her?

TOM: I'm twenty-five. It's someone else's turn. That's not unfair.

MARY: I didn't say it was.

TOM: But there's no reason for you to stay.

MARY: For someone so bright, you're incredibly dim.

TOM: What do you mean?

MARY: I met all these chinless wonders at university, arrogant idiots who think they own the world. I've never met anyone like you. So now you probably think I'm some mad stalker.

TOM: I think – I think you're round the bend.

She kisses him.

It's been a while.

MARY: Good things come to those who wait.

She kisses him again.

TOM: Maybe we should take things slowly.

MARY: To hell with that. I wore special underwear.

They begin to undress each other. TOM's mobile rings.

TOM: I'm sorry.

MARY: Ignore it.

TOM: I can't. (*He answers it.*) Yeah?… Christ!… Yeah, well leave him up there, then… Alright. Alright, I'm on my way.

MARY: Gotta go?

TOM: I don't want to.

MARY: I'll be here, Tom Connor. Chaise-longue, grapes –

TOM: Sweet melodies…

He kisses her.

SCENE 5: TOM'S HOUSE, DECEMBER, 1997

GERRY opens a bottle of Champagne.

SALLY, MARY, TOM and JANET all hold out glasses for him to fill. SALLY is wearing Oxford University sweats.

ALEX watches.

TOM: Merry Christmas, everybody.

ALL: Merry Christmas!

TOM: Sally, it's great to see you.

JANET: You look really well, lovely. Is that sweatshirt just in case you forget you're a genius, or in case we do?

SALLY: It's so you all treat me with the respect I deserve.

GERRY: As if we'd treat you otherwise.

MARY: So how is it?

SALLY: A grind. I can't believe you've graduated.

MARY: Grown-up at last.

TOM: No gap years, Sally. Do you see?

SALLY: And what are you doing with a big loser like him?

MARY: Don't know, can't shake him off.

TOM: They're ganging up on me, Alex.

ALEX: Got to be at least three to be a gang.

TOM: You got me. Would you like a glass?

ALEX: Yes, please.

GERRY: Yes?!

TOM: Special occasion. The whole family together, so to speak.

GERRY: I'll drink to that.

SALLY: So, I've got an announcement.

GERRY: Tell me you're not.

SALLY: Chance'd be a fine thing.

JANET: Watch out for medical students, Sally. They pray on the young and naïve.

GERRY: It's true.

JANET: One spiked drink and you wake up ten years later to a life of slavery and servitude.

TOM: Let the girl speak!

SALLY: Thank you. I have a job offer.

GERRY: Already?

SALLY: I mean, I have to get my degree, but that's a given, so.

JANET: Well, who with?

SALLY: BBC Television. Production assistant. I mean, the money's crap, but this is what I want to do.

JANET: Sally, that's fantastic!

SALLY: Thank you! It was ridiculously competitive, so I didn't want to say anything until I knew. But they phoned yesterday, and…it's definite.

GERRY: Well, good for you.

MARY: Will you commute? I mean, will you live here?

SALLY: I thought, oh, it doesn't matter now, I just wanted to let you know the news.

TOM: Come here! (*He gives her a big smacker.*) I'm proud of you. My genius sister!

SALLY: Thank you, Tom.

MARY: There's food next door, everyone. We did the figs in bacon like you suggested, Janet.

GERRY: Wonderful!

JANET: Did you stuff the figs with goat's cheese first?

GERRY: Leave them alone, Janet. We can't all be perfect.

JANET: We can try!

GERRY: Get in there, wench. Come and help us with the food Alex.

ALEX, GERRY and JANET exit.

TOM: (*To SALLY.*) Let me top you up.

SALLY: About that job, I should have talked to you first, I'm sorry.

TOM: Are you kidding? Best news all year.

SALLY: You've been stuck here, I know.

TOM: We've had a blast.

MARY: He met me.

SALLY: That's true. Not all bad. How's Alex?

TOM: His exhibition got in the local paper.

SALLY: And this video camera?

TOM: Loves it. Still learning, but he loves it.

SALLY: How is he at home?

TOM: Up and down. Started asking questions.

SALLY: About what?

TOM: Oh, things. Family. Abstract things. But questions are good, Gerry says. It means change.

SALLY: A couple of girlfriends asked if I'd share with them. One of them owns a place.

TOM: In London?

SALLY: I didn't give them a yes.

TOM: If it makes the job practical…

SALLY: We can talk about it.

TOM: You deserve success, Sal.

SALLY: As soon as I'm settled…

TOM: Go grab some food before Gerry scoffs the lot.

SALLY: I'm really glad you two are together. She's completely out of your league.

MARY: It's pro bono work. Charity.

TOM: (*To SALLY.*) Get out of here.

SALLY exits.

MARY: You okay?

TOM: I'm fine.

MARY: She could have been more sensitive.

TOM: Kids! Go on through.

MARY: It will happen for you, Tom.

TOM: Go on through.

MARY: I love you.

TOM: Yeah?

MARY: Yeah. You're the best man I know.

MARY exits. TOM crumples.

ACT TWO

Part I: Documenting Love

SCENE 6: GERRY'S GARDEN, SEPTEMBER, 2002

JANET contemplates the weather. GERRY enters putting on his coat.

JANET: Isn't this weather beautiful?

GERRY: Indian summer.

JANET: Driest September in a decade. So says Radio Four.

GERRY: Must be true.

JANET: Why don't we walk up the Downs?

GERRY: Do what?

JANET: There must be two good hours of sunshine left.

GERRY: I can't. I'm going to Tom's.

JANET: Oh.

GERRY: Another evening.

JANET: Yeah.

    Beat.

GERRY: What?

JANET: Nothing.

GERRY: What?

JANET: I just thought, you were at Tom's yesterday evening, maybe it was my turn tonight.

GERRY: It's not – what do you mean 'turn'?

JANET: We talked about spending a bit more time together.

GERRY: We are.

JANET: Like a normal couple.

GERRY: Another evening. Tom needs me over there.

JANET: Sure this isn't what you need?

GERRY: Oh, they're making this little film, and it's bringing all sorts of things out of Alex. I think he's changing.

JANET: We're all changing. Sarah's changing.

GERRY: It's such a crucial time for Alex.

JANET: Right.

GERRY: They need me, Janet.

JANET: Tom's got Mary. They're grown ups now.

GERRY: Why don't you go out for a walk?

JANET: I probably will.

GERRY: Take Sarah.

JANET: She's at a sleepover.

GERRY: Oh. Where?

JANET: A girl in her class.

GERRY: Which girl?

JANET: I don't know. They all look the same.

GERRY: You didn't tell me –

JANET: I did, Gerry! We had a conversation, or some semblance of a conversation, this morning. Where have you gone?

GERRY: Oh, come on, Janet. Don't be dramatic. I work bloody hard.

JANET: I know! I know that.

GERRY: All this is over a walk up the hill.

JANET: It's not over a – don't be silly, Gerry. I feel forgotten, sometimes. Sarah feels forgotten.

GERRY: I don't think that's true at all.

JANET: You're a man with two families.

GERRY: Janet.

JANET: When you're here, when you're here in body and mind, you're just like you were back at college. You know that?

GERRY: Apart from the hair.

JANET: Do you know I love it when you slap my arse?

GERRY: What?

JANET: And when you say, 'Let's get in the car and go on holiday'. And we just do.

GERRY: We did that once.

JANET: Well, I love it. But more often than not, Gerry, you're with them. Even if you're here. And you have been since their mum died.

GERRY: I have to go.

JANET: It's not natural, it's not normal.

GERRY: I was their doctor and their friend. I have a duty of care.

JANET: A duty to who, to their mum? Because I don't understand that Gerry. Where is it written? Exactly? Am I collateral damage?

GERRY: This is ridiculous.

JANET: It's been, what twelve, thirteen years since their mum died? And you still put yourself through this daily self-flagellation.

GERRY: It's not that at all.

JANET: What is it, then?

GERRY: They're like family.

JANET: You'd better go. If that's what you promised.

Beat.

GERRY: Two hours of sunlight?

JANET: Yes.

GERRY: Still time for a walk.

JANET: Yes.

GERRY: Get your wellies on, you've pulled.

SCENE 7: SALLY'S OFFICE, LONDON, SEPTEMBER, 2002

TOM sits at SALLY's desk. ALEX plays on SALLY's office chair, raising it, lowering it, and swivelling it around.

TOM: Alex. Alex. Alex.

ALEX breaks something on the chair.

Come and sit over here.

SALLY enters with documents and a cup of coffee.

SALLY: Sorry I'm late.

TOM: Nice office.

SALLY: It's alright. Did Marianna offer you tea and coffee?

ALEX: Orange juice.

SALLY: Or orange juice. Good. And did you look round town this morning?

TOM: That's this afternoon. Business first.

ALEX: We're going to Trafalgar Square.

SALLY: What do you think so far?

ALEX: It's busy.

SALLY: (*To TOM.*) Coping?

TOM: No panics yet, hey Alex?

ALEX: (*To SALLY.*) He's been very well behaved.

SALLY: How are things with Mary?

TOM: Sal, they're fine. Quit keeping us in suspense. What do you think?

SALLY: Of the material?

TOM: Of course the material.

SALLY: You know what I think. It's fantastic. You didn't tell me how much you've done.

43

TOM: We didn't realise. (*To ALEX.*) Did we?

ALEX: Just sort of did it.

TOM: Started shooting, talking to people, you know? The new camera's great. Made us feel sort of legit, didn't it?

ALEX: It's heavy.

SALLY: Looks great on screen. Those shots by the canal are just stunning.

TOM: And the editing suite's raised our game. But Alex put it together, really.

ALEX: We both did it.

SALLY: (*To ALEX.*) You talked to the old lady?

ALEX: Yeah.

TOM: She's at the nursing home down past the post office.

ALEX: She's ninety-four.

SALLY: It's a beautiful section.

TOM: She just opened up to him.

SALLY: On his own? (*To ALEX.*) You spoke to her on your own? All that stuff about her husband –

TOM: Could we show it to someone?

SALLY: What's the goal? What are we asking for?

TOM: What do you think we should ask for?

SALLY: I think we've got a programme. Can you put together a showreel? They won't watch the whole thing.

TOM: Of course.

SALLY: Alright. I'll draw up a pitch document. We have a programme about love – a series exploring the nature of love. A century of love, right? A ninety-four-year-old, right down to a four-year-old.

TOM: Will they go for it?

SALLY: I can talk to Toby, who's my exec. This is close to a BBC Four brief he's already given, except that this is better. It's original, challenging and, most importantly, made by Alex. I want to push for a meeting with Alex. Let him talk to them directly.

TOM: Talk to who?

SALLY: Toby, a couple of others. At an executive meeting.

TOM: I don't know if we can do that.

SALLY: What do you think, Alex?

TOM: Sal, come on. You know what you're asking.

SALLY: Would you talk about your ideas in front of a few people?

TOM: You don't have to, Alex.

ALEX: Don't mind talking.

SALLY: You want this to be a family thing, don't you?

TOM: That's a completely different issue.

SALLY: Alex is the angle here.

ALEX: It's not about me.

SALLY: It is.

TOM: We should focus on the content of the series.

SALLY: We should focus on it, but it's not enough to get it made. We could just be another flash in the pan production company –

TOM: Who said anything – I just thought you should see Alex's work.

SALLY: Think about the opportunity.

TOM: You mean Alex?

ALEX: Don't want this to cause an argument.

SALLY: I don't think, Alex, that what makes you different from other filmmakers is anything to be ashamed of. You've got a disability, but with it you have some extraordinary skills. Why shouldn't we get excited about that?

TOM: I understand what you're saying, Sal, but I want to make sure that we protect what Alex was searching for in the first place.

SALLY: Tom, I agree. But let it evolve. Subjective documentaries are in vogue and I think we can exploit that without losing the integrity of the piece.

ALEX: It's not about me.

SALLY: It's about all of us, isn't it?

TOM: I suppose so.

SALLY: Well, if it's about us, why not start with our impulses? I'll come down this weekend – have you got any plans?

TOM: No.

SALLY: We can set up the camera, knock back some wine and break open the taboos.

TOM: What?

SALLY: We'll talk. On camera.

TOM: I don't know, Sal.

SALLY: Do you know what your ideas about love actually are? It's meant to be an exploratory programme. Isn't it? So let's get exploring.

SCENE 8: TOM'S HOUSE, SEPTEMBER, 2002

TOM films ALEX'S face in extreme close-up and a projector beams it onto the wall behind. SALLY sits nearby with a notepad and pen.

TOM: Are you ready?

ALEX: I don't know.

TOM: I'm here for you. Tell me what you know about love.

ALEX: I don't know anything.

TOM: Just talk to the camera.

ALEX: Can see you're here. Can't think.

TOM: First thing comes into your head. Are you nervous?

ALEX: Yes.

TOM: Why?

ALEX: I don't know.

SALLY: Do you want me to go?

TOM: You don't have to go.

SALLY: Alex? I can wait outside.

ALEX: Yes.

SALLY: Would that make you feel easier?

TOM: This was supposed to be the three of us.

ALEX: Just talk to Tom.

TOM: Sal?

SALLY: It's fine.

TOM: Ten minutes.

SALLY: As long as you need.

She leaves.

TOM: Why were you shy with Sal?

ALEX: Don't know.

TOM: We've got to be honest, the three of us. That's the point of this.

ALEX: Just you and me.

TOM: I'm your brother, she's your sister. What's the difference?

ALEX: You're Tom.

TOM: Alright, Alex. Begin again?

ALEX: Begin again.

TOM: What do you know about love?

ALEX: It's a word.

TOM: A four letter word.

ALEX: Yes. Four letters.

TOM: What else?

ALEX: One word isn't enough.

TOM: How many words should we have?

ALEX: You could never have enough.

TOM: Why?

ALEX: It's in everything.

TOM: What do you mean?

ALEX: Every moment. Last week in London. Trafalgar Square. The pigeons. Watched the clouds and lost track of time. Nearly missed our train. And you said, 'Jesus, Alex, we've got to run'.

TOM: Sounds right.

ALEX: You ran through the pigeons. I followed you. You run faster than me. Suddenly the breath was knocked out of me. Lost my balance. Nearly fell over. Had to stop.

TOM: What made you lose your balance?

ALEX: Knew what it was. Knew before I turned round and saw her. You hadn't seen me stop. You'd reached the other side of the square.

TOM: What was it, Alex?

ALEX: Turned round. People walking to and fro. All trying to get somewhere. Like us. Sun playing patterns in the fountains. It caught the pigeons by surprise and hundreds of them took off into the air at once. And then. Just a moment. She was standing there. Sun in her hair. The pigeons' wings flashing. My mum. Our mum. She smiled at me. I was falling towards her. Reaching out for her. Could feel my heart split. I burnt up in front of her. Like tissue paper.

TOM puts his hand over the lens.

TOM: Stop now, Alex.

ALEX: There isn't a word for that.

TOM: Enough, now.

ALEX: The dead stay with you. Don't they?

TOM: Alex!

ALEX: They reach back. When you least expect it. Out of the corner of your eye. A flash of a pigeon's wing. You look over your shoulder. And it's love. It's the only meaning.

SCENE 9: TOM'S HOUSE, OCTOBER, 2002

ALEX films MARY.

ALEX: Do you love him?

MARY: Yes.

ALEX: How do you know?

MARY: I know.

ALEX: How?

MARY: It's an instinct. I don't know. He's your brother, Alex. This feels funny.

ALEX: Sorry. Don't have to.

MARY: No, no, it's fine. Why are you so interested in love?

ALEX: Want to capture moments of it.

MARY: Of love?

ALEX: See if it's possible.

MARY: Haven't you watched all those old love films? *Casablanca, Gone With the Wind?*

ALEX: Don't mean like acting.

MARY: You mean for real?

ALEX: I think there's a sadness. Sits next to the joy and watches.

MARY: Why do you think that?

ALEX: Something I've seen. 'Love is always hungry and can never be full.'

MARY: Have you ever loved anyone?

ALEX switches off the camera.

I didn't mean that to sound terrible.

ALEX: I love Tom. I love my mother.

MARY: I mean like a man and a woman.

ALEX: Used to watch my mum. She loved Tom. More than anything in the world. More than Sally. Watched her love him every day. Stood in the shadows. And I could see her sadness. In the corner of her eye. Like a bruise.

MARY: Love can bruise. I believe that.

ALEX: There was joy, too.

MARY: But you didn't feel it?

He shakes his head.

You'll find someone, Alex.

ALEX: Knew that if I ever fall in love, won't be able to stop falling, like falling into warm water and not wanting to come up for air, just turning and twisting and watching the bubbles wriggle upwards, knowing that in the end I'll burst to breathe. So if I feel a connection, I hold back, hold on, stop falling.

MARY: Losing control is one of the pleasures of love.

ALEX: See people touching, holding hands, walking close together, lying close together, and I think, that must be special. Really special.

MARY: Why don't you try it, then?

ALEX: Can't connect.

MARY: Do you think you connect with me?

He nods, uncertainly.

Well, I'm practically your sister. Think that means we can touch hands?

ALEX: Don't know.

MARY: Without getting confused?

ALEX: Not confused.

MARY: Alright then. Put up your hand.

ALEX puts up his open hand. MARY touches the tips of his fingers with hers.

Alright?

He nods.

No different to touching Tom, is it?

ALEX: Softer.

MARY: What about Sally?

ALEX: No.

Beat.

MARY: Maybe we should stop.

Neither of them moves.

ALEX: Remember watching you dance with Tom. In the street.

MARY: It never did snow, did it?

ALEX: Watched you dance. Thought, 'I couldn't do that'.

MARY: Let's try.

ALEX: Can't.

MARY: Slow.

She moves towards him, guiding him with her hands.

Put your hand round my waist.

He does so, tentatively, but without fear.

And now move your feet with my feet.

ALEX instantly looks down.

Keep looking at me. Let them move on their own. Alright? You're dancing.

They dance closely, in silence.

ALEX: He's very lucky, my brother.

MARY: Yes he is. I'll never stop loving him. Love is always hungry, never full.

SCENE 10: SALLY'S HOUSE, LONDON, NOVEMBER, 2002

SALLY helps JANET into the living room. They are followed by ALEX, carrying his overnight bag.

JANET: I'm so sorry.

SALLY: It's alright.

ALEX: Smells funny.

JANET: You didn't have to pick me up.

SALLY: I was driving Alex into town, anyway.

JANET: You're a sweetheart.

ALEX: Is it red wine?

SALLY: Alex!

ALEX: Smells like red wine.

JANET: (*Suddenly nauseous.*) Oh, God!

SALLY: Alright. Are you alright?

JANET: Yep. I think I'd better use your bathroom.

SALLY: Down the hall. Door at the end.

JANET: I am so sorry.

She exits.

ALEX: Bit smelly.

SALLY: Alex, you can't say that.

ALEX: She's drunk.

SALLY: Be nice to her.

ALEX: I like your flat.

SALLY: Thank you.

ALEX: Am I going to the office with you tomorrow?

SALLY: Yes, if you'd like to.

ALEX: You want me to stay here so you know I won't panic at your office.

SALLY: Alex, I don't want you to feel like you're being used. Tom and I love you and respect you. You know that, right?

ALEX: Yes.

SALLY: So, we're going to talk to some people about your filming, about how it's helped you, some of the things you're interested in, people you've met, that's all.

ALEX: And I'm going to stay here tonight?

SALLY: It was supposed to be you and me. That's what I wanted. But Janet called, and she's a good friend, so.

ALEX: Gives Tom a break, and Mary, me staying here.

SALLY: And we can talk a bit. Once Janet's passed out.

ALEX: This work, making films, it's changed things.

Enter JANET.

JANET: Much better.

SALLY: Alex, why don't you get Janet a glass of water?

JANET: Thank you.

ALEX exits.

SALLY: (*After him.*) There's mineral water in the fridge.

JANET: I didn't know who else to call. Couldn't go home. Used to know lots of people in London.

SALLY: It's fine.

JANET: You learn who your friends are, don't you?

SALLY: They just left you?

JANET: Will you call Gerry for me?

SALLY: Yes. How are you feeling?

JANET: Stupid. I bet you don't make a fool of yourself, do you?

SALLY: If only you knew.

JANET: Everything works out for you.

SALLY: That's not true.

Enter ALEX carefully carrying a glass of water.

ALEX: It's Evian.

JANET: Thank you, Alex.

SALLY: I'll make up my bed for you.

JANET: No, sofa, please.

SALLY: I'll get some sheets then.

SALLY leaves.

JANET: Thank you for my water.

ALEX: That's okay.

JANET: Why are you looking at me, Alex?

ALEX: Something different.

JANET: I look ridiculous.

ALEX: No.

JANET: I must look awful.

ALEX: No.

Beat.

JANET: So, you're enjoying all this work with Sally, then?

ALEX: Yes. It's changed things.

JANET: Who'd have thought that camera would turn out to be such a successful present?

ALEX: You look softer.

JANET: What?

ALEX: Softer. That's what's different.

JANET: Older.

ALEX: No. In the eyes.

JANET: Wrinkles.

ALEX: Your hands are shaking.

JANET: It's the booze.

ALEX: Your hair is half up half down.

JANET: Does it have sick in it?

ALEX: Like a girl's hair. Like you're a girl again. Soft. Why are you sad?

JANET: I'm not.

ALEX: You've been crying.

JANET: My friends left me sitting outside a bar on my own.

ALEX: Before they left you.

JANET: How do you know?

ALEX: Different kind of crying.

JANET: Is it, now?

ALEX: Cried on your own.

JANET: Saw my face in the mirror –

ALEX: And cried?

JANET: And cried.

ALEX: Why are you sad?

JANET: I'm not, darling. I'm not. I'm just – I'm…

ALEX: Lost.

JANET: I can't stand – I just – I can't bear who – and I don't recognise myself. I don't recognise my voice, my laugh, the snide little comments I make. I'm comatose, dreaming the old dreams, the same dreams I had when I was awake, alive. And nothing done about them. I – (*Quietly, with shame.*) Christ Almighty Jesus Christ.

ALEX leans forward and gently wipes a tear from her cheek.

ALEX: It's going to be alright. Can tell.

Part II: Hit & Run

SCENE 11: TOM'S HOUSE, DECEMBER, 2007

TOM and MARY are snuggled up on the sofa. TOM fidgets incessantly.

MARY: What's the matter?

TOM: Nothing.

MARY: Stop it, then.

TOM: What?

MARY: Stop doing that thing with your hand.

TOM: What am I doing?

MARY: What aren't you doing?

TOM: Fine. Want to go out?

MARY: Not unless you tell me what's wrong.

TOM: It's nothing.

MARY: You spoke to him less than an hour ago.

TOM: Spoke to who?

MARY: Don't give me that.

TOM: You know how many nights in his life he's spent on his own?

MARY: He's been up and down to Sally's for years now. His own place! That's a wonderful thing. He's got phones, alarm buttons, Sally's down the street, there's Homecare three days a week. And he'll be back for Christmas. He's a different person, Tom.

TOM: He is, isn't he? How did that happen?

MARY: Are you kidding?

TOM: He grew up.

MARY: You can't see it, can you?

TOM: What?

MARY: Tom, you've been brother, dad, carer, colleague, you've given him confidence, self-belief, and you've done it without question or hope of change. He's a tribute to you.

TOM: Why are you so lovely?

MARY: It's a mystery.

TOM: I think I'll give him a call, anyway.

MARY: Let him have the night. He'll call you if he needs to.

TOM: His own place! That's something, isn't it?

MARY: Yes.

TOM: A production company, another series on its way, cash in the bank, Alex on the cover of *Broadcast* –

MARY: He looked sweet.

TOM: Maybe we'll win a Bafta.

MARY: Why not? Let's have two, see if they breed.

TOM: It could happen.

MARY: It will happen. 2008 is the year of the Connors.

TOM: What if he's panicking too much to phone?

MARY: Okay, that's it.

TOM: What?

MARY: You know what day it is?

TOM: Yes.

MARY: No, you don't.

TOM: Am I missing something?

MARY: Ten years today.

TOM: You and me?

MARY: Since we…

TOM: What?

MARY: Since we established a sacred, biblical bond between man and woman.

TOM: Since we did it?

MARY: Yeah.

TOM: Ten years?

MARY: Happy anniversary.

TOM: It's not our real anniversary.

MARY: Don't be a spoilsport.

TOM: You're scheming.

MARY: I'm not.

TOM: I can see it in your eyes.

MARY: This was going to wait until our official anniversary, but seeing as you need some distraction –

TOM: What?

MARY: Let's go away.

TOM: On holiday?

MARY: Away away. Travel. Properly. We both want to, right? And we haven't been able to.

TOM: We went to Paris.

MARY: For a weekend, Tom. That's not what you used to dream about.

TOM: And Alex?

MARY: I talked to Sally.

TOM: Already?

MARY: Yes.

TOM: Without talking to me?

MARY: I'm doing this all wrong because you've rushed me into it.

TOM: I have not.

MARY: The idea is, that the travelling, Tom Connor, would be a bit more than just travelling.

TOM: What do you mean?

MARY: I mean it would be a honeymoon.

TOM: A, a honey – a what?

MARY: A long, glorious honeymoon.

TOM: Are you –

MARY: Asking you to marry me, yes.

TOM: I'm supposed to ask you.

MARY: I've been waiting ten years, you great lummox.

TOM: You want me to –

MARY: Spend the rest of your life with me.

TOM: To –

MARY: Love me and cherish me, whatever the weather.

TOM: I –

MARY: Do?

TOM: Yes.

MARY: Really?

TOM: Wait a minute, this is, what are you doing?

MARY: Getting you to agree before you have a chance to think. Tom, there's a giant hole in the earth in Mexico and you just lean over the edge with a parachute and drop down into it. I thought we might start there.

TOM: What about money?

MARY: You could let this house for a decent sum, and there's your stake in the company, and I've got a bit of money, and Mum would help us as a wedding present, and anyway, I don't want swanky hotels and expensive cocktails.

TOM: You look great in a cocktail dress.

MARY: I want to share the world with you. It's a simple thing.

TOM: You never stopped surprising me.

MARY: Boo.

TOM: What's the catch?

MARY: I'm proposing to you, and you're asking what's the catch?

TOM: You've got that look in your eye.

MARY: Okay. When we get back, if we get back and we don't end up running a beach bar in the Caribbean, which would be fine by the way –

TOM: When we get back?

MARY: I want you to have my babies. I'm thirty-two. God knows how old you are. I want a family.

TOM: That's the catch?

MARY: What do you think?

TOM: I think you should be my wife.

SCENE 12: GERRY'S HOUSE, DECEMBER, 2007

GERRY enters from outside. JANET has been waiting for him.

GERRY: I'm sorry I'm so late.

JANET: Darling! That's alright. I've just done you a bit of late dinner. And when you're finished why don't you come upstairs and I'll give you a massage.

GERRY: Really?

JANET: Don't be a bloody idiot, Gerry.

GERRY: Sorry.

JANET: I tried to phone you.

GERRY: My phone was off.

JANET: I realise that.

GERRY: I was driving.

JANET: Can't you get one of those thingies?

GERRY: I expect I can get one of those thingies, but as I don't have one I thought it best to switch off the phone. Have we got anything in the fridge?

JANET: The strychnine's on the top shelf with the pesto.

GERRY: They're tripping off the tongue tonight.

JANET: Where were you driving from? Has Tom moved to, I don't know, Vladivostok?

GERRY: No. Tom has not moved to Vladivostok. I was driving Alex up to London.

JANET: Wait for it, here it comes…

GERRY: (*Suddenly clicking.*) Oh, bugger, bugger, bugger. I was supposed to –

JANET: Take Sarah to the gig.

GERRY: Did she go?

JANET: I actually had a back-up. In case you did your disappearing act.

GERRY: So she went?

JANET: Her friend's parents.

GERRY: Good. Have fun, did she?

JANET: 'Have fun, did she?' Why can't you remember, Gerry? Why?

GERRY: It's one in the morning, I'm going to bed.

JANET: I waited, Gerry.

GERRY: Alright, what is it?

JANET: It's come to my attention that this isn't a healthy marriage.

GERRY: Maybe if you sobered up –

JANET: It's come to my attention that this marriage is a little crowded.

GERRY: Right. Blame it on Tom and Alex.

JANET: Did you love her, Gerry? Don't ask who.

GERRY: Of course I didn't.

JANET: You can tell me.

GERRY: For God's sake, it was nearly twenty years ago. She was a patient.

JANET: At what point did you stop loving me?

GERRY: I'm not getting into this.

JANET: I think I'm going to leave you.

GERRY: Are you done? Because I'm going to bed.

JANET: I think I want a divorce.

GERRY: Oh, really. On what grounds?

JANET: Take your pick. Adultery, I expect.

GERRY: For God's sake, she was a patient!

JANET: Not you, Gerry. Me.

GERRY: Adultery?

JANET: I'm seeing someone.

GERRY: No, you're not.

JANET: Ask me who.

GERRY: You're not. Are you?

JANET: Ian.

GERRY: Who?

JANET: Sarah's ballet teacher.

GERRY: Don't be daft.

JANET: Incredible. You are just so conceited.

GERRY: The ballet teacher? Since when?

JANET: Six weeks, on and off.

GERRY: Why? Why would you do that?

JANET: Gerry, for twenty years I have orbited you. Like a moon. I loved you beyond reason, beyond words. And I have never been more than a distant object floating through space.

GERRY: Ha! The ballet teacher! Does he wear his leotard? I assumed he was a bloody queen!

JANET: He's not.

GERRY: Are you still seeing him?

JANET: No.

GERRY: Does Sarah know?

JANET: Of course not. I don't think so, no.

GERRY: For fuck's sake, Janet!

JANET: You can sleep down here, if you want.

GERRY: You can bloody sleep down here. I'm having the bed.

JANET: No. You're not.

GERRY: Why would you do this? Hurt me like this?

JANET: You're an intelligent man. Work it out.

GERRY: I was never unfaithful to you.

JANET: Don't try and take the moral high ground. This was sex. There are worse ways to be unfaithful. (*Beat.*) You can leave me.

GERRY: You've got nothing. No money, Janet. What'll you do? No more appointments at the salon. No more designer clothes. You'll just be a faded beauty.

JANET: I'm already a faded beauty.

GERRY: He's practically a kid!

JANET: I sunk low.

GERRY: To hurt me?

JANET: To be held. Simple as that.

GERRY: I've driven you to it. Is that what you think? (*Beat.*) What are we going to do?

JANET: Drink?

GERRY: Janet.

JANET: I hate myself.

GERRY: Don't say that.

JANET: Oh, it's okay, I hate you too.

GERRY: I don't recognise us. Do you?

JANET: Not for years. I wish we could retrace our steps.

GERRY: I don't want to lose you.

JANET: Why do you say that now?

GERRY: Because you need looking after.

JANET: Oh, for Christ's sake.

GERRY: Because I didn't realise.

JANET: You're blind.

GERRY: I suppose I am.

JANET: There's only one way we can go on.

GERRY: No, Janet.

JANET: Without Tom, without Alex, without Sally. And you have to have to drive their mother out of your mind.

GERRY: They're family.

JANET: They're not fucking family!

GERRY: I don't know if I can.

JANET: You can try.

> *GERRY'S mobile rings. He looks at the number.*

> Don't answer it.

> *GERRY answers the phone.*

GERRY: Hi, Sally.

JANET: Unbelievable!

GERRY: (*On the phone.*) What's the matter? Slow down… When?… Is Tom there?… Okay, I'm on my way. Call me if there's any change.

> *He hangs up.*

JANET: Let me guess, the idiot savant has locked himself in a cupboard?

GERRY: Mary's been in a car accident.

JANET: Is she okay?

GERRY: She's in surgery.

JANET: Do they know –

GERRY: They're not saying.

JANET: Go.

GERRY: Will you –

JANET: I'll still be here, Gerry. Go.

SCENE 13: HOSPITAL, DECEMBER, 2007

TOM sits in a functional hospital chair. SALLY stands near him.

SALLY: Can I get you anything?

TOM: No.

SALLY: Coffee?

TOM: You should go to bed, Sally.

SALLY: I want to stay here with you.

TOM: I'm okay.

SALLY: I'm bloody not.

TOM: They said it could be hours. You shouldn't have come down, Sal. It's a long trip for you.

SALLY: It's nothing.

TOM: Taxi must have cost you a fortune.

SALLY: It doesn't matter.

TOM: Let Gerry drive you back to the house. Get some sleep.

SALLY: I'm fine. What did the police ask you?

TOM: Not much. I don't know anything, do I? Mary called me. When I got there she was unconscious. The car was upside down.

SALLY: Were they helpful, at least?

TOM: They offered me a counsellor. I said no.

SALLY: Why?

TOM: She'll be okay. She'll pull through.

SALLY: Of course she will. That's not the point.

TOM: I'm fine. Just tired.

SALLY: Any news of the other driver?

TOM: Not yet.

SALLY: How can people be so – I don't know, cowardly doesn't come near it.

TOM: Probably scared. Drunk, maybe.

SALLY: What about all your travel plans?

TOM: We can postpone that. She's strong and young. She'll be okay.

GERRY enters.

GERRY: Any news?

SALLY: Not yet. How's Clara?

GERRY: She's getting some air. She'll be back in a second.

SALLY: Poor thing.

GERRY: Has anyone talked to Alex?

TOM: There's no need to talk to Alex. She'll be okay.

GERRY: Tom, I want you to take something.

TOM: What are you talking about?

GERRY: To calm your nerves.

TOM: My nerves don't need calming.

GERRY: Tom, listen to me. You know, even if surgery is a success there's no telling what injuries she might have suffered to her brain.

SALLY: We don't need to – Gerry!

GERRY: I am praying she'll recover, of course I am, but we should moderate our expectations.

TOM: Gerry, she'll be fine. She called me from the car. She was able to use the phone.

GERRY: I know.

TOM: She told me very clearly where she was. She said she thought maybe she'd broken her legs, but she didn't mind travelling the world on crutches. She actually laughed. So. And then she said she loved me, said she'd always loved me. Since she could remember.

SALLY: Why don't they give us some news?

TOM: I rode with her in the ambulance and there was a point when she nearly woke up again. So, you see Gerry, she's going to be okay. You mustn't worry.

GERRY: Yeah. I'll find someone who knows what's going on.

GERRY exits.

SALLY: I'm sorry, Tom.

TOM: It was an accident.

SALLY: It always falls on you to be strong.

TOM: 'We're made strong by the people we love.'

SALLY: That what you tell Alex?

TOM: When he needed to hear it, yeah.

SALLY: You're a selfless man, Tom. And I've been a conceited, spoilt little girl.

TOM: Nonsense.

SALLY: It's true. Alex has made me realise that. He started asking me about Mum.

TOM: I don't want to talk about Mum.

SALLY: That's what I said. But he was asking out of concern, out of a deep love for you. At Mum's funeral –

TOM: Sal, now is not the time.

SALLY: Okay. You're right. But thank you. For holding my hand.

GERRY enters.

TOM: What? Did they say anything? She's going to be fine, right?

GERRY: Tom, I'm so sorry, she haemorrhaged. I'm so, so sorry.

TOM: What do you mean?

GERRY: They couldn't save her, Tom.

TOM: What do you mean?

GERRY: Her heart stopped beating a few moments ago. They couldn't resuscitate her. The surgeon was – I thought it was better coming from me.

TOM: Well, there's been a mistake.

GERRY: No mistake.

TOM: Who do I speak to? I'll sort this out.

GERRY: I'm so sorry.

TOM: She spoke to me. She told me she loved me. She'll be fine. They've made a mistake. That's all, Gerry.

SALLY: Tom…

GERRY: She's gone.

TOM: Right. Right, I see. I'd better talk to the surgeon, then. There'll be paperwork. Things to do. You should go home, both of you.

GERRY: I'd better find Clara.

TOM: No, I'll take care of this. I'll take care of everything.

ACT THREE
SNOWBOUND

SCENE 14: TOM'S HOUSE, MARCH, 2008

GERRY lays the table for dinner. There are a couple of bottles of wine waiting to be opened. TOM enters from the kitchen.

TOM: A snowstorm?

GERRY: That's what the weather forecast said.

TOM: Maybe they're right.

GERRY: It's bloody cold, but not a breath of wind.

TOM: A storm? Maybe they're right.

GERRY: Tom, I think you should go travelling. Not necessarily the places you'd planned to – or, or – I just think, you know, get out of this house, Tom.

TOM: Your hands are shaking.

GERRY: My hands? It's nothing. I'm tired. Sell the place. You only stayed here for Alex. Because of his 'attachment', or whatever you want to call it. He's thirty-three, he's doing well. And Sally's grown up. too.

TOM: I like it here.

GERRY: Mind if I have a Scotch?

TOM: Of course.

GERRY: You're a people person, Tom. You don't flourish in isolation. Move to the city. At least you can surround yourself there. At least there's noise, there's hubbub. Something to drown out the silence. You grow old quickly here. So old. Look at me. I'm actually twenty-five.

TOM: What's your secret?

GERRY: I moisturise. (*Drinking.*) God, this is nice. You wake up one day and you're spent. In your youth you imagine you can reach each other, but the reality is you pass each other by. And it's exhausting. Which way do dessert forks go?

TOM: I have no idea.

GERRY: Do we even need dessert forks?

TOM: This cutlery was my parents' wedding present.

GERRY: Doesn't actually answer my question, but thanks. I'm going to go for prongs to the left. Janet would know. She could snap her fingers and this table would look like the bloody Ritz. You know what I did the other morning? I left the toilet seat up.

TOM: What are you talking about?

GERRY: I left it up. To see what would happen. And to make things interesting, I did a little bit of pee on the floor. Just… swung out to the left. Enough so she'd notice.

TOM: Are you alright?

GERRY: Oh she noticed! God, it's unfair on Sarah. Poor thing. I don't know, Tom. I've woken up in a sitcom. There's never any real, any genuine – well, we passed each other by, and that's the truth.

TOM: Another whisky?

GERRY: Best not. Oh, alright. Just a drop. How are you? Is this for real or is it just bluster?

TOM: It's all under control, Gerry.

GERRY: It's only been three months, Tom. Go up to London. Stay with Sal. Are you sleeping?

TOM: Like a baby.

GERRY: Bad dreams? You're bound to get bad dreams. I remember when my dad died–

TOM: No bad dreams.

GERRY: What, then?

TOM: I don't dream.

GERRY: Nothing?

TOM: It's a blank.

GERRY: That's shock.

TOM: I don't think so.

GERRY: Table's laid.

TOM: Good. That's just as it should be.

A car pulls up outside.

GERRY: Take it easy on yourself tonight. No one's expecting you to be on best form.

TOM: There's nothing wrong with me.

GERRY: I haven't been as attentive as I should have been, for which I am ashamed, but things, well, it's been somewhat busy at home.

TOM: I never asked for your attention.

GERRY: Tom, I know. But I'm your friend.

The doorbell rings.

Could well be Janet. She's been out all afternoon. God knows what state she's in.

TOM exits to answer the door. TOM and SALLY enter.

TOM: A bottle? Thank you.

SALLY: Freezing out there. Going to snow, apparently. Hi Gerry, how are you?

GERRY: I'm fine, Sal. Good to see you.

SALLY: (*To TOM.*) You sure you're up for this tonight?

TOM: Wow. You two in cahoots?

GERRY: We're concerned.

SALLY: Exactly.

TOM: How's work, Sal?

SALLY: It's fine. Everyone misses you. Everyone's thinking about you. We're all pulling together on the workload. And there's nothing you can't do from home. If that's what's best.

GERRY: How's Alex?

SALLY: Leaps and bounds.

GERRY: Any reaction to Mary's, I mean –

SALLY: He's devastated, of course. As far as it goes. You know how it is. He disconnects. Undocks and sails off.

GERRY: Lucky him.

SALLY: Mind if I open the wine? I'm parched.

TOM: Make yourself at home. I've got things to do in the kitchen.

SALLY: Can I help?

TOM: Everything's under control.

TOM exits.

GERRY: Stuck with me.

SALLY: Always a pleasure. How's Sarah?

GERRY: Misses Mary.

SALLY: Can I ask you a question?

GERRY: What?

SALLY: Do you think this is a good idea?

GERRY: Honestly?

SALLY: Yeah, me too.

GERRY: He's acting a little – well, it's like he's talking through a vacuum. And then to organise this, it doesn't make any sense.

SALLY: And inviting Clara?

GERRY: I know.

SALLY: Have you seen her? Since the funeral?

GERRY: On and off.

SALLY: How is she?

GERRY: In bits, of course.

SALLY: Have you prescribed her anything?

GERRY: Sally…

SALLY: Sorry.

GERRY: She's very fragile.

SALLY: Her only child…

GERRY: And the violence of it.

SALLY: I know.

GERRY: Tom said she was really enthusiastic about seeing everyone tonight.

SALLY: She must be lonely.

GERRY: Did he invite Alex?

SALLY: They've barely spoken since Mary died. And then only superficial conversation. I'm afraid to get the two of them together, because you know how Alex can be. But maybe I've taken it too far. Tom's stopped asking about him.

GERRY: It's shock. It's all shock. Or denial, or something. It'll catch up with him. And when it does – (*The doorbell rings.*) That's Janet.

SALLY: I'll get it.

SALLY exits. Enter TOM.

TOM: Door?

GERRY: Sally's got it.

SALLY returns with JANET and CLARA.

JANET: Sally, you look terrific! Tom! (*To GERRY.*) Darling.

TOM: Come in, come in.

GERRY: (*To JANET.*) Nice Lunch?

JANET: Fine thanks. Work okay?

GERRY: Busy.

TOM: Dump your coats.

JANET presents a carrier bag full of booze.

JANET: Three for the price of two. I couldn't resist.

CLARA: Tom, my dear, how are you?

TOM: I'm fine.

CLARA: Thank you for inviting me.

TOM: I wanted you all here.

JANET: And we all wanted to be here.

CLARA: Smells good.

TOM: Nothing fancy.

CLARA: It's about the company tonight, I think, don't you?

SALLY: Let me pour some wine. Who's driving?

JANET: We live down the road, darling, so make mine a big one.

CLARA: I think a gentle evening is what the doctor ordered.

JANET: No, the doctor ordered a Scotch.

SALLY: Did you walk together?

CLARA: Most of the way. Didn't we.

JANET: Very pleasant.

CLARA: This weather's eerie. Everything's so still.

TOM: Sit down, everyone.

SALLY: Where do you want us?

TOM: Clara, you sit here, at the head of the table.

JANET: All very formal. Dessert forks are facing the wrong way, though.

CLARA: Thank you, Tom.

SALLY: This is lovely.

TOM: I wanted to make it a special evening.

CLARA: That's what Mary would want. And we didn't really have a wake, did we? She was a social creature.

JANET: Now, we've got too many girls. You'd better sit next to me, Tom.

GERRY, JANET, SALLY and CLARA sit down at the table.

SALLY: Is anyone short of a glass?

GERRY: Cheers!

ALL: Cheers!

The wine continues to flow freely.

TOM: Good, We're all here.

CLARA: I wouldn't want to be with anyone else. This is the closest I can get to my daughter, with all of you. (*To TOM.*) How's Alex?

TOM: You'd have to ask Sally. I'll get dinner.

TOM exits to the kitchen.

SALLY: He's very well. He's cut back on the Homecare, finally. And he's more than coping at work. Everyone fits round him, you know. He's editing at the moment. And he's got a trip planned to New York. I'm going with him, but it's a huge step. He's never been on a plane.

GERRY: Do you cook?

CLARA: Yes.

GERRY: So does Janet. One of her more attractive qualities.

CLARA: It's rather therapeutic, don't you think?

JANET: I find that depends on who you're cooking for.

CLARA: Well, I'm cooking for myself these days.

JANET: Me too, usually. Gerry was sorry to miss the recital the other week, Clara.

CLARA: Oh, that's okay. I almost cancelled. But it wouldn't have been fair on my pupils. They put so much work in to it.

SALLY: I remember my first recital.

CLARA: Piano?

SALLY: Clarinet. Squeaked my way through 'Strangers on the Shore' and fled to the ladies'. I'm sure Sarah's a much better musician.

JANET: (*Topping up everyone's glasses.*) I thought it was a beautiful recital, Clara. All those little dears. And some of them clearly without a musical bone in their body. Don't you ever get tired of it?

CLARA: Not really. I love them all.

JANET: Sarah's mad keen. Practises and practises.

CLARA: She's got a lot of instinct.

JANET: (*Flattered.*) Do you think so?

GERRY: I'm afraid I couldn't come to the recital. I had a call-out.

JANET: I always think that makes you sound like a pizza delivery boy: 'call-out'.

GERRY: The Hamptons' boy. Brain haemorrhage, as it turns out. Oh, God.

TOM enters with a bowl of pasta.

SALLY: Let me clear you a space.

TOM: (*To CLARA.*) Nothing you don't eat, is there?

CLARA: No.

TOM: I wasn't sure whether I'd asked.

CLARA: This looks…fine. I like pasta.

TOM: Lucky. It's all I can cook.

JANET: Everyone likes pasta.

TOM: Dig in, everyone.

They help themselves and eat.

CLARA: What became of that television programme you made about love?

SALLY: Two sequels since then. Our bread and butter. And some silverware for the office.

GERRY: Remind me, what did you decide – about love?

SALLY: Decide?

GERRY: Yeah, you know: love–good, bad, or waste of bloody time?

SALLY: It was explorative.

JANET: Gerry's pulling your leg, Sal. Whisky makes him funny.

GERRY: It's not the whisky, darling. I've always been funny.

JANET: Don't flatter yourself.

SALLY: (*To CLARA.*) Alex talked to people of different ages and backgrounds about their relationships –

CLARA: Alex did the interviews? I'm not sure I knew that.

SALLY: He spoke to one woman who'd lost her children in a car crash.

GERRY: Sally, I don't know –

CLARA: No, you don't have to censor yourselves.

SALLY: You can tell me to shut up.

CLARA: No, I'd like to hear.

SALLY: Well, as a young mum, this woman was driving along the motorway with her kids in the back and for a split second she drifted off, drove through the central reservation and hit a lorry. She woke up a month later to find she'd killed her family.

JANET: Top up?

CLARA: What a terrible tragedy.

SALLY: She'd never talked about it. She'd lived, I don't know, frozen in time, unable to speak. And finally she unburdened to Alex. It was the most incredible thing.

CLARA: I can imagine.

SALLY: Love had immobilised her, I suppose.

GERRY: My God, Sally, I really don't think –

CLARA: Gerry, please. I'm glad we're able to talk properly. That's why I'm here.

SALLY: The question Alex put to her at the end of the interview, he asked if she hadn't loved them so absolutely whether she might have been able to move on.

CLARA: What did she say?

SALLY: I can't remember her words, but by this point she was speaking with incredible openness and honesty. She said – what was it – that love coloured the landscape of your life; every feature, every landmark, every view. She said without it she might be able to move on but it would be alone and as if walking through snow. Life would be cold and featureless.

GERRY: If I have one criticism of programmes like yours, Sal, it's that I don't think you can make any pithy conclusions about life. Maybe love just doesn't mean anything. Maybe it's one big illusion. What do you think, Janet?

JANET kicks him under the table.

SALLY: I don't think we did make any pithy conclusions. I mean, of course there were the clichés, but once we got beyond that, to some deeper level of truth, we found that our subjects, when they talked about love, they were – how did Alex put it – they were like children isolated in tiny pools of light.

JANET: Love is loneliness.

CLARA: That can't be true.

SALLY: This is delicious, Tom, well done.

GERRY: Drink up, all!

He tops their glasses.

CLARA: (*To GERRY.*) Where's Sarah tonight?

GERRY: She's at home.

CLARA: On her own?

GERRY: Oh, she's thirteen now. She's fine on her own.

JANET: She's used to it.

CLARA: I've been a bit worried about her recently.

GERRY: Why?

CLARA: Lately she's just been awfully quiet.

SALLY: I think she was fond of Mary.

CLARA: Yes, of course.

JANET: She has moods.

GERRY: (*Pointedly.*) You think that's what it is, Janet?

TOM: (*Getting up.*) Dessert.

TOM and SALLY clear away and go into the kitchen. GERRY tops up the wine.

GERRY: (*To CLARA.*) The latest thing is that she wants to get her belly button pierced. I said out of the question, but Mum here's been giving mixed messages.–

JANET: I don't think we need to talk about mixed messages, Gerry.

GERRY: I mean, she's thirteen.

JANET: I said she could think about it for a few months and if she still wanted to –

GERRY: A probationary period. We do that in our family. We like to stew things over.

JANET: (*To CLARA.*) Anyway, Sarah's in a sulk about it.

GERRY: Actually, Clara, we've been going through a few difficulties at home.

JANET: Gerry, don't you dare.

Enter TOM and SALLY with desserts.

CLARA: Tom, let me give you a hand.

TOM: Don't you even think about standing up, Clara.

GERRY: If you'll excuse me I'm going to take up smoking.

JANET: Nobody cares.

GERRY puts on his coat and walks out.

CLARA: Oh dear.

SALLY: Everything okay?

JANET: I'm sorry. He's drunk.

CLARA: This looks nice. Is it chocolate fondant?

TOM: Yes.

CLARA: It's perfect. Look at that. Just oozes out. Did you make them?

TOM: No, I cheated. Marks & Spencer's.

SALLY: 'This is not just chocolate fondant…'

CLARA: Well, you've outdone yourself with all of it, Tom.

GERRY enters.

GERRY: Who were you with?

JANET: Gerry, for God's sake!

GERRY: This afternoon.

JANET: Friends.

GERRY: You were with him.

JANET: Don't do this.

GERRY: I knew it.

JANET: Remind me, where's the bathroom?

SALLY: It's upstairs and along the landing. It's the last door you come to.

JANET: Right.

JANET exits.

SALLY: Tom, why don't you get rid of this place? Stay with me. Put it on the market and stay with me until it's sold.

TOM: I like this place.

SALLY: You always wanted to move.

TOM: Well, now I want to stay.

SALLY: Why?

TOM: It's the family home.

SALLY: It's not the family home. You never thought that.

TOM: Not until now.

SALLY: So, what's changed your mind?

TOM: I'm in the walls.

SALLY: Why don't we call it a night? Clara, why don't I give you a lift home?

GERRY: I am so awfully sorry.

CLARA: Don't worry about it, darling.

GERRY: Mind if I fix myself a Scotch?

TOM: Of course.

SALLY: No, Tom! You've had enough, Gerry.

GERRY: Thanks.

He pours himself a drink.

Married life. Jesus. My wife's shagging the ballet teacher.

SALLY: She's what?

CLARA: (*Finishing her dessert.*) Well, that really has finished me off.

GERRY: We ballsed it up.

SALLY: What are you going to do?

GERRY: Christ, I don't know.

SALLY: Can you fix it?

GERRY: I'm still here. She's still here. More or less. But I'm not sure what exactly we're trying to fix. I remember, when I married her – Christ, I adored that woman. Worshipped the ground at her feet. And now…pools of light. Is that what Alex said?

SALLY: You should see a marriage counsellor.

GERRY: We should probably all see a counsellor. Maybe get a group discount. Why don't we call it a night, hey, Tom?

SALLY: I agree.

TOM: Come on, Gerry, eat up. Coffee yet.

GERRY: Do you think any one of us isn't on the verge of cracking? It hasn't worked out, you know, and I'm sorry. Everyone's just, we're all just…

CLARA: I packed away her pictures last week. For the moment. I couldn't bear to look at them.

SALLY: Come on, Clara. Get your coat.

CLARA: I'm fine, Sally, thank you.

SALLY: Tom, this is awful.

CLARA: It's a shame Alex couldn't come tonight.

JANET enters.

JANET: Gerry, we're leaving. We're going home.

GERRY: I'm not bloody going anywhere.

JANET: You're drunk.

GERRY: Pot, kettle, black.

JANET: I won't be humiliated, Gerry.

GERRY: Sit down.

JANET: So you can choose. You can come home, or you can stay here. Do you understand? Do you understand what that means Gerry?

GERRY: Do join us, dear. The party's really just getting started. Look at this wonderful dessert.

JANET picks up her chocolate fondant, rubs it in GERRY's face and leaves.

CLARA: I expect that was very hot, was it?

GERRY: No. No, not really. Cheers.

SALLY: Gerry, go after Janet!

GERRY: No, it's done. Should have happened years ago.

He wipes his face on his napkin.

SALLY: What about Sarah?

GERRY: It's done. All done.

CLARA: Look at us. What a mess! We should be ashamed! Oh, I'm sorry. Look at me. And now I've got mascara on your lovely napkin.

GERRY: Think this one might need a wash, too.

CLARA: Poor Mary. Such a stupid way for her to go. A series of stupid events. Driving around that corner at exactly that moment. A few seconds earlier or later, she'd be here now.

GERRY: You can't think like that.

CLARA: And if the other car, the other driver, had been looking, had been concentrating – and who knows what they were thinking about?

GERRY: You can't think – if I hadn't met her, hadn't fallen in love, so stupid, whats and ifs. That way madness lies. Going home.

SALLY: How?

GERRY: Walk.

SALLY: You can't stand. Let me call you a cab.

GERRY: No, no.

SALLY: Please.

GERRY: Nothing this time of night. Isn't bloody London.

SALLY: I'll walk you.

GERRY: Stay.

SALLY: Gerry, you're hammered. Come on, I insist.

GERRY: You're so like your mum. Thank you. Tom, I…

They exit, leaving CLARA and TOM.

CLARA: I'm sorry.

TOM: What for?

CLARA: That it didn't work out this evening.

TOM: It worked out fine.

CLARA: That awful behaviour –

CIARAN MCCONVILLE

TOM: Doesn't make any difference.

CLARA: I wanted to see you, Tom. Mary adored you so much. It means a lot.

TOM: Well. I should clear up.

CLARA: Why won't you talk to me?

TOM: What do you mean?

CLARA: We have to help each other.

TOM: I'm done with all that.

CLARA: What do you mean?

TOM: Doesn't matter.

CLARA: We have to talk about it. We have to grieve. It will help.

TOM: You believe that?

CLARA: Yes. Mary wouldn't want you to bottle it up.

TOM: And what would Mary want?

CLARA: She'd want you to live.

TOM: Well, Mary's dead, so I don't suppose it matters.

CLARA: Of course it bloody does! Go abroad. Do the things you both talked about.

TOM: Empty gestures.

CLARA: Better than staying here, on your own.

TOM: I am in the walls.

CLARA: I don't even know what that means.

TOM: This is our family home. I wasn't supposed to leave it.

CLARA: Tom, I miss her too. I feel defeated too. And will, I'm sure, for a long, long time.

TOM: You seem to be bearing up.

CLARA: I'm not. I do my best to sound strong because I owe it to Mary.

TOM: You owe it to Mary?

CLARA: I have to try, Tom. I have try and pick myself up again.

TOM: What do you imagine is going to happen?

CLARA: I imagine I'm going to feel a great deal of pain for the rest of my life, but if I could choose between this pain and not ever knowing her, I would choose pain. I would choose to love her. I need you, Tom. I need you to help me get through this.

TOM: Go home, Clara.

CLARA: I feel so incredibly alone.

TOM: Go home.

CLARA: And I've been holding on for tonight.

TOM: Go home.

CLARA: I'm begging you, Tom.

TOM: Begging me for what?

CLARA: Help me grieve.

TOM: Here's my advice: lock yourself away, and wait for the storm, because in the end, you're on your own, drawing in breath for the rest of your lonely, agonising life.

SCENE 15: CLARA'S HOUSE, MARCH, 2008

CLARA is badly bruised and wears a neck brace. She walks with a stick and her other arm around SALLY's shoulder. SALLY sits her down and helps her take off her shoes.

SALLY: Is there anything I can get you? How's your neck?

CLARA: Fine.

SALLY: Is there anyone I can call?

CLARA: No.

SALLY: Would you like me to stay the night? Or you could come to London?

CLARA: No. No.

SALLY: You mustn't blame yourself, Clara.

CLARA: I don't.

SALLY: Where were you going?

CLARA: What?

SALLY: I mean you walked home. You left while I was gone with Gerry, and your car was here, wasn't it? So you walked home and then…where were you planning to drive to?

CLARA: It doesn't matter.

SALLY: Well, it's only a car. And I expect the insurance… Do you think it was black ice? God, Clara, it could have been a lot worse.

CLARA: It was kind of you to come to the hospital.

SALLY: Gerry would have come –

CLARA: He was in no fit state. You said. It was kind of you to bring me home, but I'd like you to go, now.

SALLY: I can stay.

CLARA: Go.

SALLY: Are you alright?

CLARA: I'm through the worst, I expect. It's been a long night.

SALLY: Wind's picking up.

CLARA: I've got the heating on and I'm quite alright here.

SALLY: I'm sorry about dinner. Gerry and Janet. I mean, that was terrible behaviour.

CLARA: It doesn't matter.

SALLY: I'm really worried about Tom.

CLARA: Really.

CLARA: I thought, I don't know, that he was on the edge of something. Breaking down. Something. I don't suppose we ever really mend, do we? We all drank a lot. Tom was probably plastered, too.

CLARA: He didn't drink a thing.

SALLY: God knows what he's going through. He was so happy. And so close to – I mean, he's dreamt about travelling, well, for ever. He's ill. He needs time to recover.

CLARA: He doesn't want to recover.

SALLY: Where were you driving to?

CLARA: Why don't you drop it?

SALLY: I'm just curious.

CLARA: I know what you're getting at.

SALLY: If something happened after I left – did Tom say anything to upset you? He'd be horrified to think – it was really close, Clara. You're lucky to be here.

CLARA: Oh, for God's sake!

SALLY: He said something, didn't he?

CLARA: You haven't got the least idea! Mary was my daughter.

SALLY: I can't imagine what it must be to lose a child. I remember when Mum died, and it was so awful, because Tom sat me down and told me and there was no explanation why; it just didn't make any sense. But you build yourself up again. Slowly. This sounds kind of weird, but sometimes I wonder if Mum hadn't died whether I'd have been so successful. I don't mean that to sound arrogant or anything, but I suppose it was what I needed to push myself. And I got into Oxford, and got a great job, and ten years later, you know, I've got this unbelievable house in Battersea, and my own company, and I'm doing what I always wanted to do, I'm doing it.

CLARA: Do you ever actually stop to listen to yourself? I mean, does that mouth of yours work independently of your brain?

SALLY: I'm sorry?

CLARA: Because when you talk it just sound like a series of nothings.

SALLY: I was…saying, I built –

CLARA: You think you built yourself up again? Built yourself up on what? Your company? You've packaged your brother and sold him like a cheap circus act and I don't think you've ever felt as deeply as him, or ever wanted to.

SALLY: He's gifted.

CLARA: He's gifted. That's your excuse for being utterly vacuous, is it?

SALLY: I'm sorry, Clara, but I don't deserve that.

CLARA: You think you built yourself up?

SALLY: I think I've done alright.

CLARA: And what do I build on? She was everything I ever loved. You think you can lecture an old lady about the kind of grief I don't think you ever had, or ever will have, the courage to feel?

SALLY: I don't deserve this.

CLARA: Don't you dare talk to me about 'deserve', you selfish, selfish – Tom wants to die. Or didn't you realise that? It was his last supper. A goodbye. And none of you saw it.

SALLY: Do you know how cruel that is?

CLARA: Cruel? Ask your brother about cruel. I don't think you have any idea. God, no wonder he doesn't want to go on. Why would he when he's surrounded by people for whom love is just something to sell to their executives and make them sound clever?

SALLY: I wasn't trying to –

CLARA: Oh, stop talking. Stop it. Your success, your comfortable little life, is built on one thing. It's built on love. It's built on your brother's love. You know that. Don't you?

SALLY: Yes.

CLARA: But you don't feel it. You haven't got it in you. You come in here and talk about grief like it's something you can put on your CV. He has lost everything. I have lost everything. We have been disassembled by love. In your deepest quietest moments, you think about that. Now fuck off and leave me alone.

SCENE 16: TOM'S HOUSE, MARCH, 2008

The sound of a car stopping in a snowstorm. In the near darkness SALLY enters, covered in snow.

SALLY: Tom! God, it's freezing in here. Where's the bloody light? Tom, are you here?

TOM enters, carrying a torch.

TOM: What do you want?

SALLY: It's me. Just want to talk.

TOM: Why don't you come in? Sit down.

SALLY: Can we turn on the lights?

TOM: If you want.

SALLY: Thank you.

SALLY switches on the lights. TOM lowers the torch.

I've brought Alex.

TOM: Alright. That's alright. Why did you do that?

SALLY: I want you to talk to him.

TOM: You didn't have to do that, Sal. You know? I'm fine. It's fine.

SALLY: I tried phoning you.

TOM: Did you?

SALLY: Are you answering the phone?

TOM: Obviously not.

SALLY: You should answer the phone, Tom.

TOM: I was running a bath.

SALLY: Don't say that, don't – please, Tom. I love you. We all love you. Please.

TOM: Did you want something in particular?

SALLY: I want you to talk to Alex.

TOM: What's wrong with him?

SALLY: Nothing. He's your brother.

Enter ALEX with camera equipment, which he begins to set up.

ALEX: Hello.

TOM: Hello, bro. How are you? Are you working, writing things down, getting down those ideas?

ALEX: Was worried about you.

TOM: You mustn't worry about me, you mustn't believe a thing anyone says to you, I'm fine.

ALEX: Wanted to come.

TOM: Well, you shouldn't have. It's horrible out there.

ALEX: Want you to come home with us. Want to look after you.

TOM: (*To SALLY, laughing.*) Did you put him up to this?

SALLY: No, Tom.

SALLY leaves with a reassuring gesture to ALEX.

TOM: What are you doing, Alex?

ALEX: Want to film you.

TOM: I don't think so.

ALEX: Want you to see yourself.

TOM: I don't.

ALEX: You always film me.

TOM: It was for a project, Alex. It was years ago.

ALEX: Please let me.

ALEX starts filming.

TOM: Are you going to ask me questions?

ALEX: Yes.

TOM: Are you going to ask me what I know about love?

ALEX: Yes.

TOM: I don't want to do this, Alex.

ALEX: Why?

TOM: Because what do I know about love?

ALEX: Tell me what you know about something else.

TOM: What?

ALEX: Anything. Anything you like. Us.

TOM: No.

ALEX: Mary.

TOM: Let's not play this game.

ALEX: Mary's dead.

TOM: Yes, she is.

ALEX: Like Mum.

TOM: I suppose so.

ALEX: Mum would like it here. The stillness. Snow outside. 'Surrounded by angels.' That's what she'd say, isn't it, Tom?

TOM: I expect so.

ALEX: Mum loved you, didn't she?

TOM: She had a lot of problems, do you understand that, Alex?

ALEX: We've all got problems.

TOM: Couldn't cope with her problems.

ALEX: I was her problem.

TOM: Yes. You were her problem.

ALEX: She couldn't cope with me.

TOM: She retreated.

ALEX: Where?

TOM: Somewhere love couldn't find her. Do you understand?

ALEX: Think so.

TOM: She folded into herself until nothing could touch her.

ALEX: Are you retreating, Tom?

TOM: Did someone tell you that? Did Sal tell you that?

ALEX shakes his head.

What makes you say it, then?

ALEX: Normally you'd come over and hit me on the arm and give me a hug. Normally you'd smile.

TOM: Things aren't really normal anymore.

ALEX: Things were never normal.

TOM: I don't understand, Alex.

ALEX: Maybe I can help you.

TOM: How could you help me?

ALEX: Look after you.

TOM: Christ! Can't look after yourself, can't lead a normal, independent life, but put your hand on the wall and you feel the last hundred years, right?

ALEX: Sometimes.

TOM: Well, that's no good to me, is it?

ALEX: Why?

TOM: Don't keep asking 'why', Alex.

ALEX: How did she die?

TOM: She swerved to avoid another car and she flipped over in a ditch.

ALEX: Not Mary. Mum.

TOM: Go home. Let Sally take you home, hey?

ALEX: Can't do that.

TOM: Why? Come to rescue your mad old brother?

ALEX: How did Mum die?

TOM: What good can it possibly do to know how she died?

ALEX: Better to talk, Tom, than not to talk. How did she die?

TOM: Christ, Alex! You're relentless, aren't you?

ALEX: How did she die?

TOM: Ask your sister.

ALEX: Want you to tell me. You were the first.

TOM: First? To find her?

ALEX: It was snowing. Winter. Blowing a storm like now.

TOM: Yes, it was.

ALEX: And we dug a path in the morning before you went to school.

TOM: We were going to make a snowman.

ALEX: We were going to call him Gerry.

TOM: Were we? Sounds about right.

ALEX: But you and Sal had to go to school.

TOM: Sliding down the pavement. Putting snowballs down her back until she hit me with her bag.

ALEX: Could see there was something wrong. I mean, Mum was always different when it was just me and her.

TOM: Let's drop it, hey?

ALEX: She put my gloves on and my scarf. I said, 'I'm fifteen. I can do that.' But she just carried on. Drove me to Gerry's. Hardly said anything to him. Walked back to the car. Didn't say goodbye. Didn't look round.

TOM: It's not that she didn't care.

ALEX: What happened, Tom?

TOM: You know what happened. You're not stupid.

ALEX: When you got back from school, where was Sal?

TOM: I don't know. Some after-school class.

ALEX: Mum knew it would be you home first, didn't she?

TOM: Alex –

ALEX: Loved you. First and oldest. Left you a letter, didn't she?

TOM: (*Struck.*) What?

ALEX: She left you a letter.

TOM: Yes. I didn't see it. Not till afterwards. I just walked in, walked mud in on my trainers and swore and did my best to get it off the carpet. The light fused when I switched it on. And then, in the half-dark, I saw there was water running down from the landing. Pouring down, running down the walls. And I didn't understand. I ran upstairs and the bathroom door was ajar. The carpet was sodden. I don't know why it was then, but that was when I knew she was dead. Before I saw her. So I stand there in my wet socks and push open the door. I push it open. And she is – she is there – lying in the bath – in her underwear – and her wrists – she cut deep; God, she cut deep; I can see the workings of her arm, the tendons and the empty veins – white skin, lips blue, blood on the bath, water pink. Too late. Run to her, too late, screaming, don't know if there's any noise, but screaming, swearing, angry with her, just angry with her, the deceit, the lie, kissed me goodbye this morning, kissed me goodbye in the snow.

ALEX: She loved you. Loved you above all things.

TOM: Don't say that!

ALEX: She knew we'd be okay with you. She knew.

TOM: Why do you have to – I can't –

ALEX: We'd be okay.

TOM: I can't –

ALEX: You'd put us first.

TOM: Can't –

ALEX: If she loved you less –

TOM: Don't, don't you –

ALEX: If she loved you less –

TOM: I can't hear this!

ALEX: She wouldn't have done it.

TOM: I can't breathe, I can't –

ALEX: She'd still be alive.

TOM: I'll kill you! I'll fucking kill you!

TOM hits ALEX hard in the face, knocking him down. He pins him to the floor and, sitting on top of him, punches him again and again. ALEX lets him.

It's not my fault! It's not my fault she died! It's not my fault! I didn't want her to die! You did it! You killed her! She couldn't cope! She wasn't strong, she couldn't cope! It's not my fault!

TOM breaks down. Blood pours liberally from ALEX's mouth and nose.

God, I'm sorry I'm sorry – I can't, can't breathe, can't think –

ALEX: You're going to be alright, now.

TOM: I broke your nose.

ALEX: Doesn't matter.

TOM: I'm so sorry. I didn't mean to – I can't –

ALEX: Got to focus. Hold me.

TOM: What?

ALEX: Hold me.

The two brothers embrace.

It's going to be alright. Can tell.

TOM: I miss them, Alex. I really miss them.

ALEX: I know.

TOM: The world isn't – it isn't –

ALEX: The dead stay with us. They reach back. They never stop loving.

TOM: Don't let go.

ALEX: Won't ever let go.

Beat.

TOM: Listen to that storm. The wind, the howling wind.

ALEX: Just you and me. Safe now.

TOM: The wind, and the snow piling up against the door. All that snow.

ALEX: It will blow over. It will thaw.

The End.